Beautiful Borders

Jenny Hendy

Foreword by Paul Wagland, Editor, *More from Your Garden* magazine

**FLAME TREE
PUBLISHING**

Contents

This chapter will help you negotiate the first stages of designing and planting your ideal border. It covers distinct planting zones, weather and sunlight conditions and what the soil quality and drainage is like. Whether an existing garden or a new-build site, you'll be shown the best approach for each, and the potential problems. You will discover what plants need to keep them happy, how to prepare the ground, how to improve poor soil and the most eco-friendly ways to maintain fertility.

Tailoring planting to suit specific conditions gives far better results than planting 'blind' and simply keeping your fingers crossed. This chapter outlines what's needed to create the structural framework of trees, evergreen and deciduous shrubs, conifers and bamboos. It also covers top choices for walls and fences. If you combine the right plants, you can construct easy-care borders that will make few demands on your time. Selections of flowering and foliage perennials, ground cover plants, bulbs and annuals flesh out the border and add layer upon layer of colour and texture. Useful plants lists are also included.

This chapter considers the importance of label information such as height
and planting distance. It also looks at how to select good plants and the pros
and cons of spending more on mature specimens as opposed to buying
cheaper, smaller or untrained forms. Planting techniques for climbers,
perennials, bulbs, Mediterranean herbs, alpines and annuals are covered,
along with soil preparation and drainage improvement. Initial training and
support for climbers and wall shrubs is explained as well as tree staking and
tips for increasing rates of establishment and for efficient watering.

Follow the advice in this chapter to create bed shapes and plant groupings that work from the point
of view of proportion, seasonal interest, form and texture, as well as colour. These guidelines will help
you to achieve the look and feel you desire, whether it be cool, contemplative and harmonious or hot,
energetic and dramatic. The chapter looks at shaping and sizing new borders and how to revamp an
existing garden by restyling existing beds. It also covers backdrops and boundaries and how to
contrast plants to achieve maximum variety and colour. Each section is illustrated with handy plant
lists.

If you're gardening in extreme conditions, or have soil that seems unlikely to produce the results you've
been dreaming of, you'll find plenty of helpful pointers and encouragement in this chapter. You might

want to develop an area under trees where dry shade is an issue, or your garden is located in a windy or exposed site. Or you could be getting to grips with soils ranging from waterlogged to dry, from heavy clay to free-draining sand, from acid to alkaline. You'll be encouraged to do some research, see what's growing well locally and to use plants suited to your environment.

Border Styles 148

There are all kinds of border and planting styles and this chapter explains the different strategies and maintenance involved. You might want to try modern mixed borders to create a constantly changing display with interest throughout the year. Or if flowers are your passion, you might prefer a traditional herbaceous border or the new perennial style of planting using a mix of ornamental grasses and long-flowered herbaceous. A contemporary cottage garden border can also weave in edibles to great effect, or you might want to plant borders to attract bees, butterflies and birds. The choice is yours!

Pep Up Your Borders 180

With regular care during the spring and summer months, plants can be persuaded to bloom over a much longer period or to repeat in flushes. Regular jobs include removing fading blooms and yellowing leaves; periodic cutting back and applying mulches to ensure that plants have sufficient nutrients and moisture to sustain healthy growth. Targeted pruning and tidying is also essential. With careful planning, you can fill any seasonal border gaps with seedlings, young plants and potted bulbs. This chapter will show you how to maintain seasonal colour with hardy and cornfield annuals, spring and summer bedding, bulbs and tender perennials.

Basic Upkeep 200

This chapter deals with routine jobs such as feeding, weeding and pest prevention. Clear pruning guidelines are given for most common shrubs and climbers and you will also find advice on perennial and bulb care including cutting back herbaceous and ornamental grasses in spring, as well as lifting and dividing certain plants to keep them strong and flowering well. Maintenance needs vary depending on the time of year and the style of border, but work can be kept to a minimum by growing problem-free plants that suit the border conditions and using labour-saving techniques such as bark mulching.

Propagation 224

Raising plants from seeds and cuttings is much easier than you might think and most techniques described in this chapter don't need special equipment or facilities. In fact some propagation can be done direct in the ground. A new garden can be expensive to plant up and it's more economical to limit the initial numbers of shrubs, perennials, herbs and alpines purchased and gradually bulk them up by making divisions, taking cuttings or collecting seed after they've flowered. Collecting home-grown seed is particularly rewarding and if you have like-minded gardening friends, you can swap crops to increase your range.

Foreword

Anyone with a long-term interest in gardening will know that fashions come and go. Visit the same garden show two or three years in a row and you'll notice themes and concepts peculiar to each. Of course this makes for interesting viewing, but just as remarkable is that which remains constant from year to year.

Well-designed borders have been a feature of the best gardens for centuries, and have at times been considered the pinnacle of the plantsman's art. The challenge of displaying plants in harmony is richly complex. Not only are you matching colours and habits so that they look beautiful when first combined, but you must also plan for them to grow together. The changing seasons can transform a scheme, and providing interest all year is just as important as making that big colourful impact in high summer.

For some people this pursuit has become a lifetime's work, but with the help of this book you can quickly learn how to design, construct and care for your own perfect display. Apart from showcasing your favourite plants to their best advantage, borders can be used to form divisions, boundaries and focal points within a garden design, even to provide privacy from neighbours. In recent years we have also begun to understand the value of our gardens to birds, insects and other wildlife. A display of vibrant blooms is so much more intriguing if it is thrumming with the activity of bees and butterflies. Whether new to gardening or an old, green-fingered hand, this invaluable guide will help you get the best from your borders – a guaranteed way to make your garden a success.

Paul Wagland, Editor, *More from Your Garden* magazine

Introduction

Beds and borders are where we display most of our ornamental plants and increasingly nowadays, foodstuffs and flavourings for the kitchen. Designs and plantings work best when adapted and tailored to suit the site and soil conditions. They can be made to fit any budget and can be developed or upgraded in stages.

A Comprehensive Guide

This book is an excellent introduction for novice gardeners, starting with basic information about soil, climate and plant types and moving through to essential activities such as how to plant, train and support specimens. Horticultural jargon is kept to a minimum and common gardening activities, such as dead-heading, feeding and mulching, are explained in easy-to-follow steps. If you've never had chance to explore the principles and techniques of garden design, how to make successful plant associations and colour scheming, this book covers all you need to know to create a feast for the eyes. More experienced gardeners will find Beautiful Borders a valuable reference and sourcebook to help update, upgrade and make-over existing borders. Owners of small plots will also find tailored advice and plant suggestions.

What Kind of Border?

The ideas and advice given in the following chapters should only be considered as a guideline and it's important that you exercise your creative spirit and make a garden that appeals to you personally. Mix and match styles, bend and break colour scheming 'rules' and quite simply, grow what you fancy. You'll be presented with numerous challenges and have successes and failures along the way but the experience will be worth it and you'll gather gardening wisdom and know-how to put to good use in the future.

Before making a decision about what style of planting to go for consider the many options and advantages that beds and borders have to offer:

▶ Supply of fresh fruit and vegetables, herbs and edible flowers.

▶ Good for attracting wildlife.

▶ Flowers and foliage for cutting and arranging.

▶ Fragrance and aroma.

▶ Privacy and seclusion.

▶ Shelter from prevailing winds.

▶ Cool, leafy oasis for relaxation.

▶ Vibrant backdrop to energize a dining or entertaining area.

▶ Old-fashioned charm.

▶ Sub-tropical exotica to create a sense of holiday.

▶ Easy care, year-round interest.

▶ Wild meadow or natural woodland look.

Green Approach

Creating a garden and filling beds and borders with a wide variety of plants is one of the most environmentally beneficial things you can do and gardeners tend to be more in tune with nature and aware of the creatures that share their plot. The following areas receive special attention in the book:

▶ **Water conservation:** Use drought-tolerant plants and dry border schemes as well as techniques like mulching and targeted watering to minimize wastage.

▶ **Organic pest control:** Bees and other beneficial insects and mini-beasts can be adversely affected by the use of garden chemicals so biological control methods are favoured. They also encourage natural predators.

▶ **Biodiversity:** Grow a wide range of plants to encourage insects and select plants that offer food and shelter for all kinds of wildlife.

▶ **Recycling:** Organic waste can be converted into compost to feed and mulch the garden and shredded prunings can keep weeds at bay.

▶ **Making Fertilizers:** Use home-grown leaves and convert problem weeds into nutritious liquid feeds that have a low impact on the environment.

11

Weather Matters

The weather has a profound effect on how well plants perform from one year to the next. There are precautions you can take to help more vulnerable plants, but you may still suffer damage or losses due to a summer drought, late spring frosts or high winds. Give borderline hardy plants a fighting chance by planting them in spring in a sheltered spot receiving full sun, so that they can develop thick, frost-resistant bark and/or a resilient root system in time for winter. Keep an eye on the weather forecast and if a really cold snap seems likely, wrap up apparently well-established but tender evergreens, wall shrubs, perennials and bulbs just to be on the safe side. Gardeners in areas that rarely experience frost might get away with growing half-hardy shrubs and perennials year round and not having to lift plants like dahlia or bedding fuchsias in autumn. But they could suffer more pest problems because winters are not cold enough to kill off overwintering eggs and larvae.

Seasons and Sunshine

In this book seasons and the direction of warm or cool locations are described from the point of view of gardeners in the northern hemisphere. But if you live in the southern hemisphere, the months and directions are reversed. So early, mid and late spring (March, April, May) become (September, October, November); early, mid and late summer (June, July, August) translate to (December, January, February); early, mid and late autumn (September, October, November) is (March, April, May) and early, mid and late winter (December, January, February) in the southern hemisphere is (June, July, August). Similarly, when hot, sunny borders are described, the direction is south or west facing in the northern hemisphere but east or north facing in southern hemisphere gardens.

Note: Areas with mild winters have extended seasons and can often begin the gardening year in what the rest of us would describe as late winter.

How to Use This Book

There is a logical progression to this book that takes you from surveying and understanding your plot, through the process of planning and planting beds and borders and finally describes how to enhance displays, maintain healthy plants and soil conditions and how to propagate. However, you can dip in and out of chapters that are relevant to you at a particular time in the garden's development or use some of the many plant guides as handy shopping lists. Beautiful Borders contains a wealth of design ideas and beautiful garden images for instant inspiration.

The checklists at the end of each chapter are a useful reminder of the main points you need to bear in mind when preparing, planting and maintaining your borders and if you refer to the 'Calendar of Care' every now and then, you'll keep on top of time-sensitive tasks. It's also useful to bear in mind the following points:

- ▶ **Stick to the planting distances given:** The gaps will seem too big initially but you'll be amazed at how quickly they close up. Use hardy annuals as colourful yet inexpensive temporary fillers.
- ▶ **Do your homework:** Try to avoid impulse buying. Find out as much as you can about plants beforehand.
- ▶ **Right plant, right place:** Most plants are problem free if you give them the conditions they prefer from the outset.

Note: Various poisonous plants have been highlighted through the book but this is by no means a complete list. Some people are allergic to certain plants on contact or are affected by their irritant hairs or sap. Take care to minimize risks, especially where children are concerned.

First

Steps

Kitchen

What Kind of Border?

Give yourself time to answer this question as there are numerous considerations. If you haven't done much gardening before, planning a whole border can seem daunting. It helps if you have someone to assist in ground preparation and planting as well as maintenance, but planting styles can be adapted to suit the amount of time and help available. Start to draw together ideas for how you want the garden to look, taking inspiration from your immediate surroundings and the wider landscape.

Wish List

Even though you probably won't be able to fit everything in, it helps to draw up a list of possibilities. This might include year-round colour, seasonal features, trees and shrubs for wildlife, child-friendly plants, edibles or flowers for cutting. Overlay this with practical constraints and the amount of time and funding available.

First Steps

If you've taken over an existing garden it is worth waiting to see what comes up in the borders through the year. Garden centre staff or local horticultural colleges could help identify mystery plants. Mark the position and description of bulbs and any herbaceous plants as they die down.

Location and House Style

There's no reason why you couldn't plant
cottage garden borders in an urban setting,
but to integrate with the surroundings, you
might give paths and boundaries a
contemporary twist. On the other hand if you
live in the country, a naturalistic planting style
with fluid lines could suit. But, a preference
for structure and symmetry, especially if yours
is a period property, might steer you towards
a formal design.

Layout and Conditions

In a small or awkward space you might use
organic shapes to blur the boundaries, or, in
a very large garden, divide up the plot and
tackle it one 'room' at a time. Some situations
lend themselves to certain border styles and
garden layouts:

▶ **Windy and exposed:** Prairie-style borders using perennials and grasses.

▶ **On a slope or uneven ground:** Terracing to create a series of level planting spaces.

▶ **Damp and shady:** Naturalistic woodland style or lush bog garden plantings.

▶ **Sunny with poor, dry soil:** Mediterranean or seaside feel.

17

Surveying Your Plot

Whether taking on a new-build site or an existing garden, you'll need to thoroughly investigate the area before making decisions on how to develop it. If you have an apparently blank canvas of bare ground or turf, there might still be hidden aspects to tackle such as buried builders' rubble. In old gardens you could face boundary issues such as overgrown hedges eating up precious space or broken fence panels. Investigate soil type, drainage, sun and shade as well as exposure and note any plants to prune or remove.

Garden and Surroundings

In urban areas a garden could be hemmed in by buildings which not only cast shade but also create turbulence. Large trees or an oversized conifer hedge could also take sunlight from the garden as well as draining the ground of moisture. But think carefully before taking out a hedge as there could have been a good reason for planting it – an unpleasant view perhaps or a destructive wind.

Making a Shade Map

Even if you don't draw up a scale plan of the garden, a sketch showing where the areas of sun and shade are at different times of the day is useful in working out what to plant where.

Most likely you'll find one side or end of the garden receives several hours of sunshine either in the morning, in the middle part of the day or in the afternoon or early evening. A quick way to make a record is through a series of photographs taken every couple of hours from the same spot.

Profiling Your Soil

Dig a few test pits to see how deep the darker topsoil layer is and what is beneath it. If the hole fills with water you might have a drainage problem. Also carry out several pH tests in different areas to discover how acidic or alkaline the soil is. You can buy kits or a pH meter from garden centres.

Climate and Aspect

Exploring the local weather conditions including typical temperatures in summer and winter, the first and last likely frost dates, rainfall totals and prevailing wind direction helps build a picture of what gardening might be like in your part of the world. Local influences include aspect (the compass direction your house and garden face) and proximity to a heat source such as the sea or an urban conurbation that artificially warms the region. These factors, and others that alter the normal conditions, combine to create what's called a microclimate.

Temperature and Moisture

Areas closer to the coast are invariably warmer than inland regions in winter and the reverse can be true in summer. In winter strong winds can bring temperatures down, especially if the wind travels across a cold continental interior or blows from the poles.

Upland areas and mountain ridges cause moist air from the sea to rise and as it cools, to fall as rain. The region on the opposite side is usually dry by comparison. Gardens at higher elevations are colder than those lower down and exposure to strong winds can make the situation worse. But a sheltered valley in an upland area could have its own appreciably milder microclimate.

Climate Regions

Different countries have climate maps that are divided into regions or zones allowing you to see broadly what the minimum and maximum temperatures are. Use this information to help you select appropriately cold-hardy or even heat-tolerant plants.

Local Information

Horticultural colleges and local airports keep detailed weather information which you can often access. Garden centre and nursery staff will also be able to tell you more about local weather patterns and how they relate to gardening.

Understanding Aspect and Microclimate

Gardeners can use their knowledge of the different growing conditions in the garden to put the right plants in the right places. A favourable aspect would be ideal for tender plants or ones that need more sunlight and shelter, while a cool aspect might be used to grow shade-loving plants or hardy varieties that don't need cosseting. Strong prevailing winds or turbulence created by buildings also affects conditions at a local level.

South and West

These are the warmest aspects:

▶ **South-facing:** These borders are in sun for a large part of the day.

▶ **West-facing:** These borders receive sun all afternoon.

▶ **Frost-free:** Walls absorb the sun's energy and at night act like a storage heater, releasing heat into the air and keeping the surroundings artificially warm creating a favourable microclimate.

▶ **Drought-tolerant:** Both aspects suit sun-loving plants such as herbs and Mediterranean shrubs but shade plants may suffer from leaf scorch.

North and East

These are the coolest aspects:

▶ **North-facing:** These borders only have sun first thing in the morning and at the end of the day.

▶ **East-facing:** These borders receive morning sun.

▶ **Shady:** North borders are ideal for shade lovers but sun-loving flowers will not perform well and silver, coloured leaf or variegated plants may die or revert to all-green.

22

▶ **Hardiness required:** Tender plants that rely on the insulating effect of a warm wall during winter will suffer in north and east aspect borders.

▶ **Risk of frost:** East-facing borders will support plants that thrive in partial shade but winter- and spring-blooming shrubs like magnolia and camellia suffer bud damage during frosty periods.

Top Tip

To find out which way is north, note where the sun is when it rises (which are the sunny rooms in the morning?) and where, relative to the house and garden, it goes down in the evening (is there a spot where you sit to enjoy the last rays of sun in the garden?). The sun rises in the east and sets in the west, and north is half way between these two points.

Frost Pockets

As cold air sinks, it rolls down any slope and if it meets a barrier such as a wall or fence, it pools and increases in depth. On a frosty night this can have a devastating effect on plants that aren't fully hardy. Try to visualize where frost pockets might be in your garden and make a note to only plant hardy deciduous shrubs, climbers and herbaceous plants in borders that could be affected. Also avoid spring-flowering types as delicate blossoms are easily damaged by cold.

Understanding Soil

Soil is the most important commodity in the garden and the difference that having a reasonable depth of fertile soil can make to your success in growing plants cannot be overstated. Soil takes centuries to build up naturally and is a complex living matrix. Supporting your garden soil through good horticultural practice such as regular mulching with well-rotted manure or garden compost creates the foundation on which border plants can thrive.

Healthy Soil Profile

In fertile, drained yet moisture-retentive soils, the upper layers are teeming with life – vital micro-organisms like bacteria and fungi, microscopic invertebrates and larger mini-beasts and the most important animal of all, the earthworm. These creatures need moisture to thrive and do their job, processing raw organic matter and mixing it with the tiny sand and rock fragments.

Mutual Benefit

Beneficial soil fungi or mycorrhiza connect their own extensive mycelia with plant roots enabling the plants to absorb far more nutrients from the soil. Horticulturists and farmers deliberately inoculate root systems with mycorrhiza to help plants establish, especially on poor ground.

24

Recognizing Topsoil

This upper fertile layer is where earthworms are active. Remember:

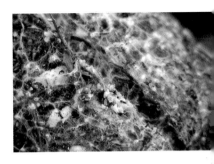

▶ It is darker than subsoil because of the incorporated organic matter and the chemical reactions that occur in the presence of oxygen.

▶ It is relatively easy to dig and may have a crumbly structure.

▶ If topsoil is shallow, don't accidentally bring subsoil to the surface through digging.

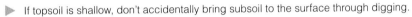

Top Tip

Many gardeners have adopted a no-dig method of gardening where the soil is disturbed as little as possible. This goes against the traditional belief that soils must be regularly dug over to incorporate manure or to break up compacted areas. Earthworms and their burrows suffer damage through digging and they will do the same job of incorporating organic matter if mulches are simply left on the surface for them.

Recognizing Subsoil

This is the layer above the bedrock and has the following features:

▶ It is appreciably paler than topsoil.

▶ There's little sign of earthworm activity (you can normally see their burrows).

▶ It may consist of solid orange-coloured clay (or grey in water-logged conditions), compacted sand particles or stone shards.

▶ It contains substances that adversely affect plant and animal growth.

25

Analysing Your Soil

Once you know what type of soil you have, how deep it is and how well drained, you can take steps to remedy any problems and to improve it. You can also tailor planting more precisely as many plants have specific requirements, especially with regard to moisture levels and acidity or alkalinity.

Simple Soil Analysis

To work out your basic soil type, pick a typical sample and work it through your fingers. You can also try to form it into a ball or roll it into a sausage shape.

Sandy Soil

▶ Is relatively light in colour

▶ Feels gritty

▶ Cannot be formed into a ball

Clay Soil

▶ Feels smooth and slippery, especially when wet

▶ Can be moulded into a ball. Heavy clay can be rolled into a sausage and bent round into a ring without it breaking

26

Loam Soil

▶ Is intermediate between clay and sand

▶ Is usually quite dark due to high amounts of organic matter

▶ Can be formed into a ball but crumbles under pressure

Acidity and Alkalinity

The pH scale runs from 1 to 14 where 1 is the most acidic and 14 the most alkaline. Neutral is pH 7 and most garden soils fall in a narrow band either side of neutral. Acid soils support ericaceous plants (ones requiring acidic conditions e.g. *Rhododendron, Pieris, Camellia*). Alkaline soils are favoured by plants that grow on chalk or limestone in the wild including many Mediterranean herbs and alpines. When sensitive plants are grown on soils outside their pH comfort zone, they suffer nutrient deficiencies.

Dry and Wet Soils

Summer drought or a climate with low rainfall can result in dry soil whereas sandy or stony soil drains very readily and cannot hold on to moisture even after heavy rain. Dry conditions cause earthworms to become inactive and they burrow deep to find moisture. Free-draining soils are naturally low in nutrients as these are washed out of the topsoil. Wet soils either suffer from poor drainage due to impermeable clay or are being fed by springs or a high water table. Saturated soils adversely affect earthworm activity and may also be low in oxygen which is essential for healthy root growth.

Calluna (heather),
an acid-loving plant

Comfrey can be used to make a
home-made fertilizer rich in potassium

Plant Nutrients

There are certain key nutrients that plants require for healthy
growth. Most of the time the roots absorb these substances in
the form of dissolved salts present in soil. Limited amounts of
certain nutrients can have a detrimental effect on growth and
various symptoms can occur such as yellow leaves with dark
green veins or reddish tints, giving clues to the problem.

The Big Three

The following have a key role to play in the growth and
development of leaves, roots, flowers and fruits:

▶ **Nitrogen:** This is necessary for the growth of leaves and shoots. Poor, thin soils lacking organic
matter and free-draining sandy soils are often lacking, as nitrogen is easily washed away after
winter rains. Symptoms involve poor growth and yellow leaves. Pelleted chicken manure
provides fast-acting nitrogen.

▶ **Phosphorus:** Contributes to root production and shoot growth. Yellow leaves and poor growth are
symptoms but deficiency is rare and symptoms could be due to nitrogen deficiency. Use
bonemeal when planting in heavy clay soils or in high rainfall areas if you suspect deficiency.

▶ **Potassium:** This vital element is involved in many important processes and affects a plant's
hardiness. Chief deficiency symptoms are poor flowering and fruiting, yellow or purple tinged
leaves and brown edges. This may be a problem on free-draining sandy or stony soils and chalk.
Feed with high potassium fertilizers like tomato food or home-made diluted comfrey liquor.

Understanding Fertilizer Packets

You will find the varying amounts of nitrogen (N), phosphorus (P) and potassium (K) in fertilizer described as the NPK ratio. A so-called balanced fertilizer might have a ratio of 7:7:7.

Micro-nutrients

Other elements are required by plants in trace amounts and are referred to as micro-nutrients or trace elements. These include iron and magnesium, boron and manganese. Many commercially produced fertilizers and tonics list trace elements in addition to nitrogen, phosphorus and potassium.

Feeding Organically

Mulches of well-rotted animal manure or garden compost are naturally rich in micro-nutrients and if compost heaps are kept under cover to keep the rain from washing away more soluble salts, they can also be relied on to supply nitrogen, phosphorus and potassium. You could also make your own liquid fertilzer from comfrey or nettles.

Improving Your Soil

Adding bulky organic matter is one of the best ways to improve the condition and fertility of soil but in urban areas it can be difficult to get hold of sufficient quantities. Garden centres do sell manure in bags but you'd need transport as these are heavy. Making your own compost is a good alternative if you have room for a bin or heap.

Bulky Organics

Mulches of manure or compost as well as other materials like seaweed or ground, composted bark add natural chemicals that help to bind fine clay particles to create the all-important crumb structure. In addition the action of micro-organisms and earthworms together with the sponge-like qualities of decayed plant matter, make soils more moisture-retentive and fertile.

Compost Making

Follow these guidelines to make perfect compost:

▶ **Brown layers:** Add thin layers of 'brown' material (carbon rich) e.g. ripped-up cardboard and newspaper, finely chopped-up twigs, fallen leaves from deciduous trees (not walnut or oak) and animal bedding such as straw and wood shavings.

▶ **Green layers:** Alternate with thin layers of 'green material' (nitrogen rich) such as grass clippings, fruit and vegetable peelings, leafy garden waste and annual weeds like nettles (excluding seed heads).

▶ **Entry for worms:** Sit the bin or enclosure on bare ground (so that composting worms can enter) and cover base with twigs for drainage.

▶ **Insulate:** Cover the bin or heap to keep compost warm and dark.

▶ **Quick compost:** Water if dry and turn as regularly as you can to speed up decomposition.

Other Additives

Extremes in pH cause problems for plants, compromising their ability to absorb certain nutrients. It isn't practical to turn alkaline soils acidic so that you can grow your favourite rhododendron, for example, but you can 'sweeten' acid soils with calcified seaweed or horticultural lime (provided you aren't growing acid-lovers). On thin, chalky soils you can improve the organic content and acidify it slightly with manure and iron sulphate. This allows you to grow a wider range of plants and lessen problems like iron and manganese

chlorosis (yellowing of leaves). Heavy acidic clays can be broken down and improved with horticultural lime. See also page 128.

Top Tip
Do not add horticultural lime at the same time as manure as this releases ammonia and wastes valuable nitrogen.

31

Preparing a Border

Once you've decided where a new border will be and have mapped out the perimeter, you have some preparation to do before planting it up. Adapting an existing border is a little more complicated. If you extend a planted border into lawn or paving for example, you many need to loosen and improve the compacted soil and add organic matter and fertilizer to increase fertility. You'll also need to move a number of the short-growing plants forward from the old section to the new.

How to Upgrade an Existing Border

This depends on how old or overgrown the bed is and whether there's a perennial weed problem. Hopefully you will have already identified the majority of plants and made decisions about which ones to move, cut back or take out. The best time to tackle moving plants and most pruning jobs is between autumn and spring, missing out any frosty or snowy periods.

Dealing with Old Shrubs

Happily many old, large and unproductive shrubs such as mock orange, viburnum and spiraea can be rejuvenated through pruning and this drastic cutting also brings them back into scale with other border plants. You might not get any flowers on plants that bloom on last year's growth but the shrub should recover its rhythm quickly. Try the following:

▶ **Cut back:** Reduce the height and width and then cut to a low framework of branches. Try to retain some natural form rather than cutting stems off at the same level.

▶ **Thin out:** Remove any dead wood and thin branches causing congestion. The aim is to let in air and light and stimulate growth of dormant buds.

▶ **Timing:** Cut back hardy evergreens such as rhododendron and cherry laurel in late winter.

▶ **Feeding:** Apply a general fertilizer in the spring to boost growth.

Rejuvenating Perennials

In a well established or rather neglected mixed border you'll discover that some more vigorous perennials have taken liberties. Reduce their volume, weed them out from between other plants and discard the remainder (do not compost). Other perennials may need rejuvenating:

▶ Look for plants with dead, woody centres surrounded by more vigorous growth.

▶ Lift and separate off the younger outer clumps. Discard the centre.

▶ Replenish soil, incorporating garden compost and general fertilizer, before replanting.

33

Preparing a New Border

On new-build sites, you may not have very much topsoil and the ground underneath could have been compacted by heavy machinery causing drainage problems. Dig a few test pits to see what the situation is. You may need to import more topsoil (check pH levels afterwards). Whether breaking new ground or digging up an established lawn, new plants benefit from copious quantities of organic matter.

Buried Rubble

As you dig new borders you might discover buried rubbish, timber, rafts of concrete, bricks and other rubble – perhaps enough to warrant hiring a small skip. Make up any shortfall with additional good-quality topsoil.

Underneath the Lawn

After skimming off turf as thinly as possible, turn over the ground to a spade's depth and break up any large, solid clods. At the same time work in garden compost or well-rotted manure and a dressing of general fertilizer such as fish, blood and bone.

Top Tip

Turn turf into topsoil by piling pieces grass-side-down and covering with opaque plastic sheeting for a year.

Checklist

▶ **Wish list:** Collect ideas including favourite plants, seasonal highlights and border styles.

▶ **Current plants:** Mark and identify existing border plants.

▶ **Your site:** List positive attributes and shortcomings of the site plus time available for maintenance, to see which style works best.

▶ **Shade map:** Make a map of the garden showing parts the sun reaches during the day.

▶ **Conditions:** Dig several holes to look at soil conditions e.g. drainage, how easy to dig, earthworm content, buried material. Find out soil pH using a kit or meter.

▶ **Aspect:** Locate compass points relative to the house to work out the warm, sunny and protected planting spots and cool, shady border areas.

▶ **Weather:** Gather local climate and weather information including your climate zone or region.

▶ **Micro-climate:** Identify microclimate conditions e.g. frost pockets, shelter from a tall hedge, warmth from a sunny wall.

▶ **Soil:** Discover soil type e.g. clay, sand, loam, chalk, poor and stony, poorly drained or dry. Note depth of topsoil and what the subsoil looks like.

▶ **Breaking ground:** Prepare new borders, removing buried rubble, breaking up compaction and adding additional topsoil if necessary.

▶ **Border makeover:** Upgrade existing borders by pruning shrubs and climbers, rejuvenating perennials and re-organizing planting.

▶ **Enrich soil:** Improve border soils with bulky organic matter and fertilizer.

Choosing Plants

Selecting Plants

Even experienced gardeners can find the wide range of plants available in nurseries and garden centres overwhelming. But if you go about it in the right way, shopping for plants can be very enjoyable. Take your time and don't just plump for plants because they have pretty flowers or colourful leaves. Combine what you know about the conditions in your garden, how much space is available and the design styles you are drawn to, in order to pick plants that will thrive and satisfy.

Wise Buys

The good news is that many of the best plants have been given some kind of award and you can find most of the information you need to make informed selections in reference books, nursery catalogues, gardening magazines and on the internet. It's also very useful to get some local inspiration and advice (*see* pages 120–21). After doing your homework, make a shopping list to avoid impulse buying.

Time Factor

These days it's not unusual to move house fairy regularly. Take into account how long it might be before the plant you have in mind reaches maturity and flowers – some magnolias can take years. Ask yourself the following questions:

▶ **Time span:** Will this plant do what I want it to in the time I'm here?

▶ **Plant development:** What shape and size will it be after five or ten years? (trees and shrubs often look different at maturity).

▶ **Speed of growth:** How quickly does it grow? (Mix instant impact purchases with longer term investments if you aren't sure how long you'll be staying).

Magnolia can take a long time to reach maturity and flower

Making Your Purchase

You can buy plants from lots of different outlets now, not just garden centres and home improvement stores. Small specialist nurseries can be inspiring places to visit and you can usually get expert advice from them. Ask around locally as some nurseries aren't easy to find. Take a handy reference guide with you when shopping. Read plant labels carefully for advice on growing conditions and dimensions and if buying mail order or online, look at more than one picture of the plant to get a better idea of its habit and overall effect.

Structural Planting

Deciduous and evergreen trees, larger conifers, shrubs, columnar bamboos and hedging form the permanent framework to a garden and as well as defining the space, also have other functions such as creating shelter and privacy, adding seasonal colour and creating a foil for flowers. In smaller gardens especially it is vital to make selections that work with the scale of your plot and that won't overwhelm the space a few years down the line.

Choosing Trees and Backdrop Plants

Many garden owners are nervous about adding trees as they worry about them getting too big, causing damage or blocking out the light. But there are trees to suit any space and they can add airy height to a border, still leaving room below for shrubs and perennials. The shape of a tree and the colour of its foliage or bark can add greatly to the scene and many have seasonal features such as ornamental fruits, autumn or spring leaf colour as well as blossom.

Picking the Right Shape and Size

Trees may be narrowly upright (fastigiate); round- or flame-headed, spreading, or weeping. Slender trees, pencil-slim conifers and columnar bamboos are useful in restricted spaces. Remember the nearer a tree is to the onlooker, the more background it blocks out. A small, round-headed tree strategically placed in a border could add just as much privacy as a larger tree planted on the boundary.

Trees for Small Gardens

If you have a small plot, try the following:

▶ *Acer palmatum* 'Osakazuki'
▶ *Amelanchier lamarckii* (snowy mespilus)
▶ *Cercis canadensis* 'Forest Pansy'
▶ *Malus* 'Evereste'
▶ *Prunus subhirtella* 'Autumnalis Rosea'
▶ *Sorbus vilmorinii*

Acer palmatum

Shrubs for Flowers

Flowering shrubs often have a big impact in the border when they are in bloom. There are evergreen and deciduous types, ones that flower in a particular season or that carry on for months. Where space is restricted, there are many dwarf and low-growing cultivars to choose from and for deep beds, plants that reach almost tree-like proportions. Fragrance is a bonus; some winter shrubs produce a surprisingly powerful perfume from tiny blooms.

Did you know?

Ornamental trees are frequently grafted onto a rootstock – you'll see a swelling towards the base. If the top part dies, the specimen may be replaced by the tree on which it was grafted. Rootstocks of variegated or coloured leaf trees sometime throw up plain shoots.

Seasonal Show

Long before most perennials come into bloom, winter- and spring-flowering shrubs take the stage. Some like forsythia put on a brief but spectacular show and are the centre of attention surrounded by early bulbs and carpeting plants. Shrubs that bloom at specific times of year help to define the seasons,

Hydrangea

from the red camellias (acid soil) and fragrant pink viburnums of winter to the lilacs and mock oranges of early summer and the hydrangeas and fuchsias that mark the beginning of autumn.

Long-flowering Shrubs

Aside from the highly productive bush roses, a number of hardy shrubs flower for months and are of great value in mixed borders. If you have reasonably moisture-retentive ground the hydrangeas offer a wealth of long-flowering specimens some of which are listed below. Try:

- *Abelia x grandiflora*
- *Fuchsia* 'Mrs Popple'
- *Hebe* 'Midsummer Beauty'
- *Hydrangea* 'Preziosa' and others
- *Hydrangea arborescens* 'Annabelle'
- *Hydrangea paniculata* 'Pink Diamond'
- *Hypericum* 'Hidcote'
- *Lavandula pedunculata* subsp. *pedunculata*

Forsythia

Roses in the Border

Many of the so-called old roses are ravishing both in terms of looks and fragrance but they may only bloom once. English roses have a similar appearance but will repeat and often have better disease resistance. Bush roses (floribunda or cluster-flowered,

Top Tip

Several winter- and spring-flowering shrubs require acid soil so check your pH before you buy.

42

and hybrid tea or large-flowered) bloom in flushes from early summer through till autumn provided they are well fed. There are compact forms of these varieties too, including patio and miniature roses which are ideal for narrow beds. Try:

Shrub

▶ *Rosa* 'Blanche Double de Coubert'
▶ *Rosa* 'Marguerite Hilling'
▶ *Rosa* 'Cornelia'
▶ *Rosa* 'Lady Emma Hamilton'
▶ *Rosa* 'L.D. Braithwaite'

Bush

▶ *Rosa* 'Arthur Bell'
▶ *Rosa* 'Blessings'
▶ *Rosa* 'Champagne Moments'
▶ *Rosa* 'Ice Cream'
▶ *Rosa* 'Margaret Merrill'
▶ *Rosa* 'Royal William'
▶ *Rosa* 'Warm Wishes'

Foliage Shrubs and Bamboos

Shrubs grown for their brightly variegated leaves or attractive

Hybrid tea bush rose

Floribunda bush rose

43

Choisya (Mexican Orange)

evergreen foliage provide long-lasting interest and can also bolster specific colour schemes. Some achieve tree-like proportions if left to grow so check dimensions before you buy or be prepared to prune. Larger plants can provide useful screening though and some, like columnar bamboos, can take the place of trees, adding privacy in smaller plots.

Evergreen Variety

Evergreens like cherry laurel, yew and shrubby honeysuckle make useful hedging. Some noted for their flowers such as the winter flowering *Mahonia x media* cultivars or Mexican orange (*Choisya*) also have beautifully shaped, glossy leaves. A selection of the best for coloured or variegated foliage, several of which light up shady borders include:

- ▶ *Aucuba japonica* 'Crotonifolia' (spotted laurel) (female)
- ▶ *Buxus sempervirens* 'Elegantissima' (variegated box)
- ▶ *Choisya ternata* 'Sundance'
- ▶ *Elaeagnus x ebbingei* 'Gilt Edge'
- ▶ *Escallonia laevis* 'Gold Brian' and 'Gold Ellen'
- ▶ *Euonymus fortunei* 'Emerald 'n' Gold'
- ▶ *Leucothoe* 'Scarletta' (acid soil)
- ▶ *Lonicera nitida* 'Bagessen's Gold'
- ▶ *Phormium tenax* Purpureum Group (New Zealand flax)
- ▶ *Photinia x fraseri* 'Red Robin'

Grass Giants

Bamboos are actually evergreen grasses and there are many

Top Tip
Some conifers (cultivars of pines, cedars, firs and spruces) make fine garden trees when in their youthful or juvenile phase but will eventually become too large for most suburban locations. It's perfectly OK to cut the tree down and replace it when still small enough to handle.

beautiful selections for gardens from variegated groundcover types to stately columns, some with coloured or striped stems. A few unruly individuals earned bamboos a bad reputation but the following graceful specimens are an asset in any garden, adding a touch of junglescent exotica:

Phyllostachys aurea

- *Phyllostachys aurea*
- *P. aureosulcata f. aureocaulis*
- *P. nigra*
- *Fargesia nitida*
- *F. murielae*
- *F. m.* 'Simba' (more compact)

Dark and Light

The following shrubs have gold or deep purple leaves that add bright and dark highlights:

Did You Know?

One of the best variegated hollies *Ilex x altaclarenis* 'Golden King' is actually female and the gold and white variegated *I. aquifolium* 'Golden Queen' and 'Silver Queen' are both male!

- *Berberis thunbergii* 'Atropurpurea' and the dwarf 'Baguatelle' (barberry)
- *Catalpa bignonioides* 'Aurea' (golden Indian bean tree)
- *Cotinus coggygria* 'Royal Purple' and *C. c.* 'Golden Spirit' (smoke bush)
- *Leycesteria formosa* 'Golden Lanterns' (golden pheasant berry)
- *Sambucus nigra* 'Aurea' and *S. n.* 'Eva' (syn. 'Black Lace')
- *Sambucus racemosa* 'Sutherland Gold'
- *Spiraea japonica* 'Goldflame'
- *Weigela florida* 'Foliis Purpureis'

45

Nandina domestica
(Chinese sacred
bamboo)

Cornus alba
'Elegantissima'
(variegated dogwood)

Sparkling Variegation

Newly opening foliage of many variegated deciduous shrubs is particularly bright and colourful. The maple (*Acer*) and weigela listed below have additional pink tints:

▶ *Acer negundo* 'Flamingo'
▶ *Berberis thunbergii* 'Rose Glow' (barberry)
▶ *Cornus alba* 'Spaethii' and 'Elegantissima' (variegated dogwood)
▶ *Cornus contraversa* 'Variegata'
▶ *Sambucus nigra* 'Marginata' (variegated black elder)
▶ *Weigela florida* 'Florida Variegata'

Shrubs for Seasonal Colour

Autumn leaf displays can be just as vivid as those produced by flowers and coloured foliage and turning leaves are a welcome focus in cold gardens where evergreen colour is harder to maintain. Overlay with glistening berries and late perennials, and autumn borders develop a real richness. As leaves fall, some shrubs reveal a previously hidden bonus – strikingly coloured stems.

Autumn Leaf Colour

The following shrubs have reliable displays of red, orange and yellow tints:

▶ *Acer palmatum* (Japanese maple)
▶ *Aronia melanocarpa* and 'Autumn Magic' (chokeberry)
▶ *Berberis thunbergii* (barberry)

46

▶ *Cotinus coggygria* cultivars (smoke bush)

▶ *Enkianthus campanulatus* (acid soil)

▶ *Euonymus alata* (firebush)

▶ *Fothergilla major*

▶ *Hamamellis x intermedia* e.g. 'Arnold Promise' (witch hazel)

▶ *Nandina domestica* (Chinese sacred bamboo) – evergreen

▶ *Vaccinium spp.* (blueberry) - acid soil

Berry Bounty

Many rose family shrubs and trees have attractive fruits including firethorn (*Pyracantha*) (red, orange and yellow – choose scab and fireblight-resistant forms); cotoneaster (from back of the border types to creeping alpines – mainly red but also yellow and pink) and rowan trees (*Sorbus*) with red, orange, pink or white berries. Single flowered *Rosa rugosa* cultivars produce big red hips and the shrub rose 'Geranium', elegant scarlet fruits. Other colourful berries are found on holly (red or yellow); snowberry (*Symphoricarpos*) – white, pink or purple; *Viburnum opulus* (translucent red or yellow) and the acid-requiring *Gaultheria* (red, pink, purple, white).

Winter Stems

Light up a sunny winter bed with the following:

▶ *Cornus alba* 'Sibirica' (scarlet); *C. sericea* 'Flaviramea' (yellow); *C. sanguinea* 'Midwinter Fire' (mixed) (dogwood)

▶ *Rubus cockburnianus* and the yellow leaved 'Goldenvale'; *Rubus thibetanus* (white-stemmed bramble)

▶ *Salix alba var vitellina* 'Britzensis' (coral bark willow)

Ilex (holly)

47

Climbers and Wall Shrubs

The size and growth rate of climbers and wall shrubs varies enormously and it is vital that you do your homework before you go shopping, noting what area or structure you need to cover, and having a list of possible candidates. Don't wait too long to make an impact on a large brick wall but, equally, try to avoid having to wrestle for control in a small border with an over-vigorous vine. Although flowers are a major attraction, with some climbers, foliage or fruit is the main talking point.

Flowering Climbers

There are all kinds of flowering species and cultivars for border backdrop walls, fences and trellis panels including some with intoxicating perfume like star jasmine (*Trachelospermum*), late Dutch honeysuckle (*Lonicera periclymenum* 'Serotina') and white Chinese wisteria (*Wisteria sinensis* 'Alba'). Climbing hydrangea (*Hydrangea anomala* subsp. *petiolaris*) is superb on a shady wall but reigning supreme are clematis and roses, prized for their long-flowering period and showy blooms.

Lonicera (honeysuckle)

Clematis for All Seasons

The genus *Clematis* is very diverse but separating them out by flowering time is a useful aid in selection.

Winter and Spring

All except the sculpted *C. armandii* have ferny foliage and delicate bell flowers, double in *C. macropetala:*

▶ *C. alpina* and cultivars
▶ *C. armandii* and cultivars e.g. 'Apple Blossom' (fragrant, evergreen)
▶ *C. cirrhosa* var. *balearica* and 'Wisley Cream' and C. c. var. *purpurascens* 'Freckles' (fragrant, evergreen)
▶ *C. macropetala* and cultivars e.g 'Markham's Pink'

Early Summer

Try *Clematis montana* (very vigorous, tolerant of more exposed or shady aspects) e.g. 'Elizabeth' and 'Tetrarose' (pink, fragrant).The sumptuous early, large-flowered types are compact and work well on obelisks. Most have a second flush in late summer or autumn and are susceptible to clematis wilt. You can also try the following:

Clematis montana

▶ *C.* 'Arctic Queen' (double)
▶ *C.* 'Guernsey Cream'
▶ *C.* 'Nelly Moser'
▶ *C.* 'Niobe'
▶ *C.* 'Rebecca' (repeats well)
▶ *C.* 'The President'
▶ *C.* 'Vyvyan Pennell' (double on first flowering)

49

Clematis viticella

Clematis orientalis

Late Summer and Autumn

Relatively small-flowered but prolific and wilt-free Viticella Group, for example:

▶ C. 'Alba Luxurians'
▶ C. 'Betty Corning'
▶ C. 'Étoile Violette'
▶ C. 'Kermesina'
▶ C. 'Madame Julia Correvon'
▶ C. 'Royal Velours'

Also try the elegant bell-flowered *Clematis* Texensis types:

▶ C. 'Etoile Rose'
▶ C. 'Gravetye Beauty'
▶ C. 'Princess Diana'

Plus the large, late-flowered hybrids:

▶ C. ' Jackmanii'
▶ C. 'Gipsy Queen'
▶ C. 'Hagley Hybrid'
▶ C. 'Huldine'
▶ C. 'Perle d'Azur'
▶ C. 'Polish Spirit'
▶ C. 'Rouge Cardinal'
▶ C. 'Ville de Lyon'

You will also get prolific late summer and autumn displays from
C. orientalis and *C. tangutica* (yellow bell flowers, ornamental
seed heads).

Climbing Roses

Try combining climbing roses with large, late-flowered clematis.
The following rose types are repeat flowering climbers:

- ▶ 'Aloha'
- ▶ 'Compassion'
- ▶ 'Dublin Bay'
- ▶ 'Gertrude Jekyll'
- ▶ 'The New Dawn'

Foliage Climbers and Wall Shrubs

You won't usually find an area in garden centres
devoted to wall shrubs. Plants will be dotted
through the shrubs and trees section and
also mixed in with climbers. Wall shrubs use
the support and shelter of a wall or fence
but don't tend to need as much tying in as climbers. Along with foliage climbers,
they can be invaluable as a backdrop for flowering border displays. A warm,
sheltered wall also allows you to grow more unusual species and cultivars but you
might need to visit larger garden centres or specialist nurseries to buy them.

Humulus lupulus
(golden hop)

51

Variegated Ivy

Climbers for Foliage

The following add colour and form and contrast nicely with flowers. The foliage of hop, *Ampelopsis* and *Parthenocissus* help to light up shade. Large-leaved *Vitis coignetiae* adds a sub-tropical feel and in sun develops rich red and purple colour:

▶ *Ampelopsis brevipedunculata* 'Elegans'
▶ *Humulus lupulus* 'Aureus' (golden hop)
▶ *Parthenocissus henryana*
▶ *Vitis coignetiae*
▶ *Vitis vinifera* 'Purpurea' (purple grape vine)

Evergreen Cover

More vigorous evergreen climbers and wall shrubs soften large areas of wall. Variegated ivies e.g. white-splashed *Hedera colchica* 'Dentata Variegata' and yellow-centred 'Sulphur Heart' are ideal and wildlife friendly. Prune to control size. Train firethorn, *Pyracantha*, formally on wires to keep it slimline. Try variegated ivy, the

Magnolia grandiflora

Top Tip

Avoid east-facing positions for spring-flowering, wall-trained shrubs including magnolia and camellia, as frosted buds can be damaged by morning sun melting them too quickly.

winter catkin bearing *Garrya elliptica* 'James Roof' and firethorn as a backdrop for a shady or winter interest border. For sun, plant cultivars of *Pittosporum tenuifolium*, the white-edged *Viburnum tinus* 'Variegatum' and fig (*Ficus carica*).

Flowering Wall Shrubs

On acid soils in shade try evergreens like camellia and in sun, white-flowered eucryphias e.g. *E. x nymansensis* 'Nymansay' or *Magnolia grandiflora* 'Exmouth'. For early flowers on alkaline soils in sun, or against a north wall train flowering quince (*Chaenomeles speciosa* and cultivars).

For other sunny spots try the following:

- *Abutilon x suntense*
- *Azara microphylla*
- *Carpenteria californica*
- *Ceanothus*
- *Cytisus battandieri* (moroccan broom)
- *Prunus mume* 'Beni-chidori'
- *Solanum crispum* 'Glasnevin' (potato vine)
- *Solanum laxum* 'Album'

Ceanothus tumbles down a wall

53

Herbaceous Perennials

Hardy flowering or foliage plants that die back in winter to emerge again in spring are incredibly useful in cold or exposed sites as they spend winters safely tucked up below ground, especially when covered with an insulating layer of dry bark. Herbaceous perennials and bulbs normally have a fast growth rate and starting with a few mixed pots you can often build up substantial swathes of single varieties in just a few years, really making an impact.

Leucanthemum x superbum
(Shasta daisy)

Flowers to Fit

You can buy plants that vary in size from towering, back-of-the-border types to mini or compact versions of old favourites like Shasta daisy (*Leucanthemum x superbum*). Selected varieties are often superior in flower form, habit and colour choice to straight species but not always as robust. Look for proof of garden-worthiness on labels e.g. AGM (Award of Gardening Merit) and check other vital statistics.

Getting the Timing Right

Appealing to impulse buyers, garden centres tend to have once-flowering plants like peonies, or seasonal bloomers such as autumn-flowering asters, in stock only when in bloom and looking their best. So to plant late summer or autumn interest plants in spring, or spring and early summer bloomers in autumn, when soil conditions are ideal, you may need to go to specialists who carry a full range throughout the growing season.

Top Performers

The following hardy summer- and autumn-flowering perennials are well worth a spot in the border.

- ▶ *Achillea millefolium* cultivars (yarrow)
- ▶ *Anemone x hybrida* 'Honorine Jobert' (Japanese anemone)
- ▶ *Aster x frikartii* 'Monch'
- ▶ *Campanula lactiflora* 'Loddon Anna'
- ▶ *Campanula percisifolia* (peach leaved bellflower)
- ▶ *Echinacea purpurea* (purple cone flower)
- ▶ *Geranium* 'Ann Folkard' (cranesbill)
- ▶ *Geranium* 'Johnson's Blue', 'Brookside' and 'Jolly Bee' (cranesbill)
- ▶ *Helenium* 'Moerheim Beauty' (sneezeweed)
- ▶ *Iris sibirica*
- ▶ *Knautia* 'Melton Pastels'
- ▶ *Leucanthemum x superbum* – double, single, white and yellow flowered (Shasta daisy)
- ▶ *Penstemon* 'Andenken an Friedrich Hahn'
- ▶ *Phlox paniculata* e.g. 'Starfire' (border phlox)
- ▶ *Rudbeckia fulgida var. sullivantii* 'Goldsturm' (black-eyed Susan)
- ▶ *Salvia x superba; S. nemorosa* and *S. x sylvestris* cultivars (ornamental sage)
- ▶ *Sedum* 'Herbstfreude' ('Autumn Joy')
- ▶ *Sidalcea* e.g. 'Elsie Heugh'
- ▶ *Teucrium hircanicum* 'Purple Tails'

55

Foliage Effects

Some herbaceous and evergreen foliage plants have as much to contribute as flowering varieties and the varied texture and colour can enhance the look of flowers as well as strengthening colour schemes. Leaves are more enduring and it makes sense to add a good percentage of quality foliage plants like heuchera or hosta as well as evergreen plants noted for their flowers including penstemon and elephant's ears (*Bergenia*).

Shade Plants

In shady borders it can be difficult to maintain colour and interest beyond spring as many summer-flowering perennials do best in full sun. But there are beautiful and colourful shade-loving foliage plants. Some even have attractive flowers too. Try:

▶ *Hosta*: The range includes variegated and plain green, gold or blue-grey leaved cultivars; miniatures for raised beds to large architectural plants. Some like 'Royal Standard' are also noted for their flowers.

▶ *Heuchera*: Most of these colourful, mound-forming evergreens are tolerant of partial shade, especially the lighter purples, purples-overlaid-with-silver like 'Silver Scrolls' or greens with purple net-veining.

▶ *x Heucherella*: (man-made hybrid between *Heuchera* and *Tiarella*) Beautifully shaped evergreen maple-like or lobed leaves often with a darker centre. 'Stoplight' is bright gold-green with dark brown blotch; 'Kimono' and 'Tapestry', green with bronze markings; 'Sweet Tea', orange-bronze; 'Quicksilver', purple overlaid with silver. They all have attractive flowers.

▶ *Carex oshimensis*: 'Evergold' – mound of evergreen lime-green-to-gold striped, grassy leaves.

▶ *Brunnera macrophylla*: Particularly white-variegated forms like 'Jack Frost', which has pretty blue spring flowers.

Silverlings

Silver-leaved perennials are the perfect foil for white and pastel-coloured blooms but can also lighten dark, rich schemes. Some of the best in this category are the mugworts such as *Artemisia ludoviciana* 'Valerie Finnis'. For striking architectural form add a cardoon (*Cynara cardunculus*) with large, jaggedly-cut leaves that make a bold focus.

Herb Foliage

If you want to add colourful foliage that you can also use in the kitchen, several culinary herbs fit the bill. For deep bronze filigree plumes grow the tall bronze fennel (*Foeniculum vulgare*) 'Purpureum' (select the darkest individuals when it self-seeds and discard the rest).
Purple sage (*Salvia officinalis* 'Purpurascens') is a reliable border edging for sunny well-drained sites and 'Icterina' has yellow variegation.

Ferns

Ancient 'dinosaur' plants, ferns are the ultimate choice for shade and perfect partners for the broad, solid leaves of hostas. Noted for their finely-cut foliage, ferns have a reputation for being delicate, but many garden selections are pretty robust, some tolerating a range of conditions.

Cynara cardunculus (cardoon)

57

Asplenium scolopendrium
(hart's tongue fern)

Choosing Ferns

The following is a list of garden-worthy ferns split according to their preferred situation and type but all work well in a mixed border. Deciduous ferns are particularly striking in spring when the new croziers unfurl.

Deciduous, tolerating well-drained soils in deep shade:

▶ *Athyrium filix-femina* (lady fern)
▶ *Dryopteris filix-mas* and forms (male fern)

Deciduous for moisture-retentive soils in sun:

▶ *Blechnum chilense*

Deciduous for moist soils in shade:

▶ *Dryopteris affinis* 'Cristata' (scaly male fern) (syn. The King)
▶ *Matteuccia struthiopteris* (shuttlecock fern)
▶ *Osmunda regalis* (royal fern) – attractive cinnamon fertile fronds

Evergreens for shade:

▶ *Asplenium scolopendrium* (hart's tongue fern) – best on alkaline soil
▶ *Dryopteris erythrosora* (copper shield fern) – new growths coppery pink
▶ *Polystichum aculeatum* (hard shield fern)
▶ *Polystichum setiferum* and forms (soft shield fern)

Ornamental Grasses

Grasses are increasingly popular and with good reason. There is a huge range to choose from with cultivars to suit many different border situations. Several tall-flowering types continue to look good into winter and evergreen grasses and sedges (*Carex*) provide colour and textural contrast all year.

Flowering Grasses

The following flowering grasses work well in mixed or herbaceous borders in full sun:

- *Calamagrostis x acutiflora* 'Karl Foerster' (feather reed grass)
- *Miscanthus sinensis* e.g. 'Kleine Silberspinne', 'Kleine Fontäne'
- *Panicum virgatum* 'Warrior' and others (switch grass)
- *Pennisetum alopecuroides* 'Hameln' (fountain grass)
- *Stipa gigantea* (golden oats) and *Stipa tenuissima* (feather grass)

Pennisetum alopecuroides 'Hameln' (fountain grass)

Grasses and Sedges for Foliage Effect

Try the following white- or yellow-variegated grasses; blue-leaved evergreen sun-lovers and silver- or bronze-leaved evergreen sedges (*Carex*):

- *Calamagrostis x acutiflora* 'Overdam'
- *Carex buchananii Helictotrichon sempervirens* (blue oat grass)
- *Carex comans* bronze-leaved
- *Carex flagellifera*
- *Carex* 'Frosted Curls'
- *Festuca glauca* 'Blaufuchs' ('Blue Fox') (blue fescue)
- *Hakonechloa macra* 'Aureola'
- *Miscanthus sinensis* 'Morning Light' (silver grass) and 'Zebrinus' (zebra grass)

59

Ground Cover Plants

Covering bare ground with plants reduces weeds as seedlings have fewer places to germinate. It helps stabilize light soils and is beneficial to wildlife. Creating a tapestry of different textures and colours adds another dimension to shrub and mixed borders. If you include some evergreen plants, beds will look good throughout the winter. You can use a range of plants from dwarf hardy shrubs to creeping alpines and perennials and low growing grasses and sedges. In larger areas under trees and on banks, you might use spreading evergreen shrubs and conifers.

Choosing the Right Plant

Be wary when buying ground cover that you don't inadvertently introduce a plant that will quickly take over and become weed like. This could be more of a problem on light, friable soils where roots, runners and rhizomes can spread more quickly.

Shady Ground Cover

The following perennials are useful for covering ground in shady areas both in terms of attractive leaves and flowering displays. Blend swathes of single varieties with grass-like foliage (e.g. *Hakonechloa, Liriope, Carex, Ophiopogon*) together with broader-leaved plants to maximize textural contrast and underplant with spring bulbs.

Epimedium
(barrenwort)

▶ *Ajuga reptans* 'Catlin's Giant' (bugle)
▶ *Brunnera macrophylla*

▶ *Carex* 'Frosted Curls'

▶ *Epimedium* (barrenwort)

▶ *Euphorbia amygdaloides var robbiae* (wood spurge)

▶ *Geranium macrorrhizum* 'White-Ness' (cranesbill)

▶ *Hakonechloa macra* 'Aureola'

▶ *Heuchera* (some, *see* page 56)

▶ *Liriope muscari* (lily turf) x *Heucherella* (*see* page 56)

▶ *Persicaria affinis* 'Superba'

▶ *Symphytum* 'Hidcote Blue' (comfrey)

▶ *Symphytum x uplandicum* 'Variegatum'

▶ *Tiarella* 'Pink Skyrocket' and 'Pink Brushes'

▶ *Vinca minor* (plain and variegated leaf cultivars e.g. 'Illumination')

▶ *Waldsteinia ternata*

Helianthemum nummularium (rock rose cultivar)

Alpines and Sun Lovers

Look in the alpine and perennial sections of garden centres for the following drought-tolerant groundcover plants to use on raised beds and retaining walls and as foreground planting for well-drained, sunny borders:

▶ *Acaena microphylla* e.g. 'Kupferteppich' (New Zealand burr)

▶ *Artemisia stellariana* 'Boughton Silver'

▶ *Cerastium tomentosum* (snow-in-summer) – invasive

▶ *Helianthemum nummularium* cultivars (rock rose)

▶ *Ophiopogon planiscapus* 'Nigrescens' (black mondo grass)

▶ *Rhodanthemum hosmariense*

▶ *Sedum spathulifolium* 'Purpureum'

▶ *Stachys byzantinum* 'Silver Carpet' (lamb's ears)

61

Hardy Bulbs

Spring-flowering bulbs are some of the easiest and most rewarding plants to grow whether you buy them as dry bulbs in late summer and autumn, or potted up and just coming into flower in spring. Bulbs are the harbingers of spring; depending on the weather some start to appear in late winter. Dwarf bulbs take up little room and push up through ground cover plants like heathers or cover bare soil beneath deciduous shrubs and trees. Taller kinds work well with early perennials and spring bedding.

Buying and Planting

Buy spring- and autumn-flowering bulbs as soon as they come into the shops (*see* page 85 for what to look for when buying). Plant small bulbs and autumn bloomers in late summer and leave tulips until mid to late autumn. When buying mail order, you normally select from a range of bulb sizes. The bigger the better in terms of flower quality but larger grades are more expensive.

Spring Flowers

Tulips and daffodils have so many cultivars that they are organized into a number of named groups corresponding to flowering time and structure. For example dwarf early flowering daffodils like 'February Gold' with swept back petals are in the Cyclamineus Group. Use the following list as a guide.

Naturalizing Bulbs

Some dwarf species self-seed readily whilst others bulk up if planted
with enough room between bulbs (suitable types marked with *).
Naturalized bulbs form drifts beneath trees and in shrub borders.
Plant snowdrops, bluebells and cyclamen 'in the green' (*see* page 87).

Summer Bulbs

Bulbs like ornamental onions (*Allium*) and the blue-flowered quamash
(*Camassia quamash*) provide interest as the tulips fade and before
summer herbaceous plants come into bloom. Later in summer, hardy hybrid lilies make a bold, bright
statement in mixed borders and some like the elegant white *Lilium regale*, also add fragrance.

Lilies for Borders

Plant lily bulbs direct in the border in autumn or spring or start off in pots. There's a huge
range, from short bedding types for the front of a border to tall, trumpet-flowered or
Turk's cap hybrids for the back. Incorporate plentiful bulky organic matter prior to
planting.

Ornamental Onions

Allium hollandicum and its hybrid 'Purple Sensation' are easy to please, tolerating dry
soils and light shade and like most, producing ornamental seed heads. They look good
in naturalistic schemes and cottage borders. There are many other drum-stick headed
alliums with larger blooms including 'Globemaster' and 'Gladiator'. For short, large-
headed, silvery purple flowers at the front of a sunny border try *Allium christophii*. For the
best value, plant dry bulbs in autumn.

63

Spring Flowers

Late Winter Blooms

*Chionodoxa luceliae**

Crocus chrysanthus e.g. 'Cream Beauty'

*Crocus tommasinianus**

Crocus vernus e.g. 'Pickwick' (Dutch crocus)*

Cyclamen coum *

Galanthus nivalis (snowdrop)*

Iris reticulata e.g. 'Joyce', 'Harmony'

Narcissus 'Tête à Tête'*

*Scilla siberica**

Turk's cap lily

Mid Spring

Hyacinthus (hyacinth)

Muscari armeniacum (grape hyacinth)*

Narcissus 'Cheerfulness'

Narcissus 'February Gold'*

Narcissus 'Jetfire'*

Narcissus poeticus var. *recurvus*

Tulipa (Fosteriana Group e.g. 'Purissima')

Tulipa (Greigii Group e.g. 'Red Riding Hood')

Tulipa (Single early Group e.g. 'Apricot Beauty')

Tulipa (Triumph Group e.g. 'Shirley')

Tulipa praestans 'Fusilier'

Late Spring

Narcissus 'Hawera'

Narcissus 'Sweetness'

Tulipa (Double late Group e.g. 'Angelique')

Tulipa (Lily flowered Group e.g. 'China Pink')

Tulipa (Single late Group e.g.'Queen of Night')

* See overleaf

Seasonal Plants

You can buy a range of spring and summer bedding and patio plants from home improvement stores and supermarkets but for a wider selection go to garden centres and nurseries. Mail order seed companies also sell seedlings, plugs and plantlets of many summer-flowering seasonal plants including new varieties, but you need to get your orders in as soon as the catalogues are available in autumn, to guarantee delivery in spring. You will also need a light, frost-free space to grow them on until it is safe to plant them out.

The Range

All kinds of seasonal plants are useful for bolstering border colour schemes and for filling gaps between permanent plants. For ideas *see* pages 192–198. Plant breeders are constantly improving the flowering and colour range of hardy and half-hardy bedding so don't be afraid to try new varieties. Although most bedding is discarded at the end of the season, especially if you don't have greenhouse facilities, it does represent good value since flowering and foliage displays, especially of summer bedding, continues for months.

Summer Bulbs

Summer bulbs is a blanket term that include corms of plants

Solenostemon (coleus)

Forget-me-nots

like gladioli and tubers e.g. dahlia. Dry bulbs are available from early spring in garden centres and DIY stores and you can also buy by mail order. From mid summer, potted foliage and flowering plants such as canna lilies, pineapple lily and dahlias come into garden centres ready to plant.

Seasonal Foliage

The following temporary foliage plants, all except coleus, are drought-tolerant and useful for working into summer borders as a foil for flowers:

- ▶ *Helichrysum petiolare* – silver
- ▶ *Helichrysum petiolare* 'Limelight' – limegreen
- ▶ *Pelargonium* (pot geranium) – multi-coloured, gold or white variegated
- ▶ *Plectranthus madagascariensis* 'Variegated Mintleaf' – white variegated
- ▶ *Senecio cineraria* (cineraria) – silver
- ▶ *Solenostemon* (coleus) – multi-coloured

Spring Bedding

In autumn, hardy spring bedding arrives including traditional hardy biennials like wallflowers, forget-me-nots, double daisies and hardy primulas (e.g. Wanda Hybrids) and polyanthus. Wallflowers are often sold in bare-root bundles. Soak them before planting to revive the foliage.

Canna lily

66

Checklist

▶ **Ground work:** Before buying plants check dimensions, flowering time and site requirements.

▶ **Fast and slow:** Mix plants for instant effect with those slower to mature.

▶ **Trees:** Choose appropriately shaped trees that will not overwhelm the space. Use to frame views, provide privacy and create seasonal interest.

▶ **Soil:** Check pH requirements, especially for winter and spring shrubs.

▶ **Evergreens:** Select evergreens including coloured leaf and variegated types, conifers and bamboos for year-round interest.

▶ **Climbers and shelter:** Cover walls and fences and add height mid border with reliable flowering climbers like clematis and modern roses. Grow tender evergreen and flowering shrubs on warm, sheltered walls.

▶ **Light and shade:** Pick flowering and foliage perennials to suit light soils and sunny spots. Grow shade-tolerant ferns, variegated shrubs and woodland perennials in shady borders.

▶ **Easy care:** Mix ornamental grasses with flowering herbaceous for natural-looking, easy-care plantings. Use ground-cover plants to save labour around shrubs and trees.

▶ **Bulbs:** Plant bulbs in late summer/autumn for displays from late winter to early summer.

▶ **Gaps:** Fill border gaps in summer using half-hardy annual bedding, tender perennials and bulbs.

67

The
Basics

Growing Trees

There are trees to suit every size of garden and many that have a range of features including colourful foliage, ornamental fruits or attractive bark. From a design standpoint, trees are an essential component of the garden's 3D structure and along with shrubs and taller plants help to frame the space and define its proportions. Even in a tiny plot, a well planted and nurtured tree gives pleasure for years to come so it pays to give it the best start.

Buying a Tree

Although you can buy a reasonable selection from garden centres, it is worth visiting specialist nurseries for an expanded range where you can get expert advice on picking the right tree for the spot you have in mind. Some growers focus on native varieties and will discuss aspect and soil type before suggesting the best selection for your wildlife area.

Container Grown

You can plant these at any time of year and trees will stay in their containers for some months after purchase with regular watering. When choosing trees look for:

▶ **Age:** Check for evidence that the tree has not been in its pot too long e.g. exposed surface roots, weedy compost and excessive roots through drainage holes.

▶ **Structure:** Choose a well-balanced head with clearly defined 'leader' (main vertical shoot).

▶ **Healthy growth:** watch out for dead or broken branches and signs of pests or disease.

Bare-root

Bare-root trees are ones that are lifted during the dormant season. Roots are covered in plastic (hence the alternative name 'root-wrapped'). 'Heel in' or bury roots in a spare piece of ground to insulate from frost if you cannot plant them immediately. Bare-root trees are usually cheaper, with a better root system than container grown ones.

What Size?

Trees are sold in various sizes. Whips (young trees) often establish faster than older, larger specimens and are useful for shelter belts planted to protect borders from wind damage.

▶ **Whips:** One-year-old plants from seed or cuttings with a single stem and few side branches. 'Feathers' are slightly older versions with more side branches. 'Maidens' are also whips but here the tree is grafted onto a rootstock.

▶ **Half-standards:** Trees with a clear stem of up to 1.2 –1.5 m (4–5 ft) beneath the head and which are suitable for most small to medium-sized gardens.

▶ **Standards:** These trees have a clear trunk of 1.8 m (6 ft).

Top Tip

At planting time bury a flexible plastic tube with perforations beneath the root ball, leaving the end sticking up several centimetres above ground. This enables you to feed water directly to the roots using a watering can.

Tree Planting

Trees produce a large root system so prepare an area at least 90 cm (3 ft) diameter prior to planting. Dig over and incorporate several wheelbarrow loads of well-rotted manure or garden compost to a spade's depth. Locate trees where they won't interfere with drains or house foundations (*see* Trees for Small Gardens page 41). Willow (*Salix*) and poplar (*Populus*) have a minimum planting distance of 30 m (100 ft) from buildings

Hole Preparation and Planting

After soaking (submerge roots using a large plastic trug), dig a hole several centimetres larger all round than the rootball. Pour two or three buckets of water into the base. With bare-root plants, spread the roots out, don't bend them to fit. Gently loosen or tease out roots of container-

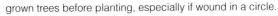

grown trees before planting, especially if wound in a circle.

Check compost surface is at the same level as surrounding soil (lay a bamboo cane across hole). Back-fill with excavated soil mixed with manure or compost. Firm with your foot, holding the trunk upright.

Aiding Establishment

After copious watering, using a bucket if necessary, to help settle soil round the roots, mulch with a tree mat or plastic sheet of 60–90 cm (2–3 ft) diameter to prevent root competition from weeds, help conserve moisture and increase rate of establishment. Peg down then camouflage with chipped bark. Protect from rabbits by fitting a spiral plastic tree guard starting just below ground level.

Staking Methods

Whips and small, untrained trees rarely need staking – just use a bamboo cane in exposed sites. With bare-root half-standard and standard trees, push a tree stake in between the roots, close to the trunk at planting time. Secure with a tree tie. To avoid damaging container-grown tree roots, after planting, drive a tree stake into the ground diagonally. Tree stakes should hold the bottom third of the stem steady but allow the top two thirds to flex in the wind, helping to build strength.

Growing Shrubs

Shrubs, including conifers and roses, form the backbone of the modern mixed border. Blending deciduous and evergreen kinds ensures year-round structure and interest. There are shrubs to suit virtually any ground conditions and microclimates and it makes sense to concentrate on ones likely to do well in your area. If you want to test your horticultural skills and pick tender shrubs, bear in mind that they do better planted in spring, allowing sufficient time to toughen up after spending the whole summer and autumn in the ground, building a large, resilient root system.

When and What to Buy

Garden centres sell container-grown shrubs all year round and if you are prepared to water while they become established, theoretically you could plant at any time. But conifers, most broad-leaved evergreens and shrubby Mediterranean herbs are best planted mid spring, after the worst of the frost is over. Wind strips moisture from the leaves and if the ground is frozen solid, plants are unable to replace it. The cold, wet soils of winter are also potentially damaging for borderline hardy plants that require sharp drainage and sun.

Mature Specimens

Occasionally it is worth splashing out on a large specimen shrub. Colourful flowering or foliage evergreens, conifers, bamboos, topiary specimens as well as wall shrubs or climbers ready-trained on a frame, are likely candidates. The trick is keeping up with watering whilst the roots establish and staking to prevent wind rock.

Bare-root Roses and Hedging

Most ornamental shrubs, with the exception of roses, are sold as container-grown plants but deciduous hedging classically becomes available in late autumn, usually in the form of bundles of rooted plants. These are considerably cheaper than buying the potted equivalent. Occasionally larger hardy evergreen hedging plant specimens like conifers, laurel and box are available with netting-wrapped root balls. If you are not able to plant bare-root hedging or roses straight away, water and heel in to a spare piece of ground or vegetable plot.

Bare-root plants are the most economical for hedge planting

Preparing the Site

Whether planting several shrubs at a time or singly, prepare the general area by digging over, weeding and improving the soil. Add plentiful organic matter e.g. well-rotted manure and a general fertilizer e.g. pelleted chicken manure or fish, blood and bone.

Planting and Aftercare

Shrubs are planted in a similar manner to trees. The addition of moisture-retentive organic matter is especially important in areas under overhanging tree branches, near walls and fences or where soil is particularly thin, poor or free-draining. When planting a hedge, dig a trench deeper and wider than required and fill the base with a mix of well-rotted manure and soil to provide a moisture-retentive reservoir.

Dig a generous planting hole.

Planting and Firming In

Make a hole as for trees (*see* left) and if soil is compacted, fork the sides and base to encourage root penetration. Plunge water then plant at same level as surrounding soil. Firm large specimens with your foot, otherwise use your hands. Water thoroughly and mulch.

Aiding Establishment

There are several ways to help plants settle in to their new bed:

▶ **Watering:** Create a shallow depression around the shrub, edged with a rim of moulded soil. This captures water and allows it to soak in.

▶ **Staking:** Stake larger plants and erect a wind break around evergreens and conifers on exposed sites.

▶ **Pruning:** Cut back branches of deciduous shrubs moderately hard at planting time to take pressure off the root system.

Success with Climbers and Wall Shrubs

These 'vertical gardening' plants can be grown in a number of different situations, not just against walls and fences. Most climbers are shrubby though some like golden hop (*Humulus lupulus* 'Aureus') are herbaceous and others, tender annuals. All need support of some kind and in the case of frost-sensitive wall shrubs, a warm, protected spot.

76

Climbing Strategies

Knowing how a plant climbs helps you design the best support framework. Some common strategies are:

▶ **Scrambling:** long, whip-like stems push up over other plants, sometimes held in place by backward facing thorns e.g. climbing roses and ramblers.

▶ **Twining:** stem twists round any support it touches. Depending on species, twining is clockwise or anti-clockwise e.g. jasmine (*Jasminum officinale*), honeysuckle (*Lonicera periclymenum*), wisteria.

▶ **Tendril Climbing:** plants include sweet and everlasting pea (*Lathyrus*). Clematis leaf stems act like tendrils, winding around wires.

▶ **Self-clinging:** pads of 'sticky' adventitious stem roots adhere to surface e.g. climbing hydrangea (*Hydrangea anomala petiolaris*) and ivy (*Hedera*). Chinese Virginia creeper (*Parthenocissus henryana*) has tendrils with disc-like suckers.

Planting Climbers and Wall Shrubs

Taking time to prepare the ground next to walls and fences properly and providing adequate support is well worth the effort. When buying, read the label to check for ultimate height and spread or you may unwittingly be taking home a monster. Only climbing roses are sold bare root or root wrapped during the dormant season. Climbers are usually sold in long pots with stems clustered around canes. Pick plants with several strong stems bearing healthy foliage or plentiful buds.

Sweet peas have tendrils

Cascading wisteria blooms

Good preparation helps climbers
establish in difficult situations

Wall and Fence Planting

Counteract the drying effects of the rain shadow by
incorporating copious quantities of bulky organic matter.

▶ Aim to plant at least 45 cm (18 in) away from the support,
which should miss any concrete wall footings.

▶ Dig a generous hole for the root ball and remove any
builders' rubble.

▶ Tilt the plant so that the canes touch the support
framework. Plant at the same level as surrounding soil,
firm with hands and water thoroughly.

▶ A shallow, dish-shaped moulding of the soil around the
plant helps capture water so that it can soak down
where needed.

Early Training

Undo the stems from the bundle after planting and
separate them out. Re-attach to a fan of bamboo canes,
guiding the climber onto the supports. Fanning out also
encourages better flowering and greater wall coverage.
If planting to climb an obelisk, gently wind the stems
round in a shallow spiral to ensure good leaf and
flower distribution.

Providing Wall Support

The following methods can be used to give climbers and wall shrubs a suitable framework:

▶ Set horizontal lines of galvanized training wire 45 cm (18 in) apart using screwed-in vine eyes to hold the wires away from the wall. Clematis plants enjoy an overlay of vertical wires forming a grid.

▶ Attach trellis panels to wooden battens, keeping panels about 4 cm (1 1/2 in) from the wall.

▶ Clip on lengths of plastic clematis mesh using the screw-in attachments provided.

How to Plant Shrubby Alpines and Herbs

In sunny gardens where the soil is well drained or even dry, this group of plants is invaluable for foreground planting in borders, especially along path or patio edges where the plants can be allowed to sprawl artfully. Fragrant and aromatic herbs including lavenders, prostrate rosemary and thymes are especially welcome in this kind of location. Shrubby herbs and alpines like Helianthemum cultivars also

Clematis need the support of wires or trellis

make valuable additions to raised beds and some alpines look spectacular cascading down over the edge of a retaining wall.

Extra Drainage

The critical factor to success is sharp drainage so if the ground is a little on the heavy side in places, dig in barrow loads of coarse grit or gravel and also create a slightly raised profile, either by shaping the bed to have a domed profile, and planting on the higher areas, or creating a low edging that can be filled with extra soil (*see* Raised Beds page 96). Position beds in full sun.

Create sharp drainage for drought-tolerant herbs and alpines

Top Tip

Always buy named, grafted wisteria plants (you will see a bulge at the base of the plant) as seed-raised plants may take many years to flower.

Mulching

Winter wet is a killer for many alpines and Mediterranean herbs and these drought-tolerant plants benefit from a surface mulch of decorative gravel or stone chippings applied after planting and watering the bed. Lift the stems and foliage and work right underneath. This helps to protect the crown from rotting and also sets off the plants, many of which look more at home surrounded by stone rather than soil.

Planting Through a Membrane

For a low-maintenance bed that won't need watering or weeding, plant shrubby alpines and herbs through a porous weed matting. You can buy this off the roll at garden centres. First ensure the area is level as undulations may cause water to puddle. Lay out the fabric and fold over any cut edges that might fray. Secure with 'pins' of bent galvanized fencing wire or metal tent pegs. Plant as follows:

▶ Set out plants in their pots and draw round with chalk before removing.

▶ Cut cross-shapes with scissors or a craft knife and peel back fabric.

▶ Plant and replace fabric round neck of plant.

▶ Remove excess soil with a brush.

▶ Water in and mulch with gravel.

Helianthemum spreads to form a carpet – ideal for planting through a membrane

Growing Flowers

Annual and perennial blooms, including bulbs, add vibrant colour to borders from spring through until autumn and are an essential element of any colourful garden. Most herbaceous perennials require similar conditions to grow well, including moisture-retentive yet well-drained soil and a good supply of nutrients to support their flowering or foliage display. It is important to find out as much information as you can on the plants you buy, not only so that you can arrange them to best effect but also so that you can match the right plant to the right spot.

Rudbeckia (black-eyed Susan)

Buying and Planting Perennials

Border perennials, though usually herbaceous, can sometimes be evergreen. They are grown mainly for their blooms or for foliage effect. Plant labels show dimensions, flowering time and growing conditions but you can often get clues to a plant's behaviour when buying. For example, if a plant appears to be 'escaping' through the drainage holes or over the rim, it's likely to be a rampant spreader, ideal for providing ground cover beneath shrubs.

When and How to Plant

You can plant at any time during the growing season although autumn and spring is ideal since there is plentiful rainfall. Pick plants with abundant healthy foliage. Preferably choose small potted plants that are not already in flower as these establish quicker. Large pot specimen plants in flower e.g. ornamental grasses are an exception.

▶ Prepare ground for planting, adding a general fertilizer like fish, blood and bone and preferably copious bulky organic matter.

▶ Pre-soak plants by plunging in a bucket of water.

▶ Mark the position of a group of plants using their pots as markers.

▶ Plant, with the compost surface level with surrounding soil.

▶ Firm in with hands, water thoroughly.

Lily-of-the-valley

Special Cases

Some perennials are best planted a little deeper than normal, taking care not to bury lower leaves. These include:

▶ Colourful-leaved *Heuchera* and *x Heucherella* cultivars and elephant's ears (*Bergenia*) that tend to grow proud of the ground.

▶ Moisture-loving types e.g. *Ligularia*, hosta, *Rodgersia*.

▶ Lily-of-the-valley – set pots several centimetres deeper to bury the young shoots.

Avoid deep planting with:

▶ **Peony:** plants stop flowering.

▶ **Bearded iris:** the rhizomes need exposure to sun, plus sharp drainage.

▶ **Blanket flower** (*Gaillardia*) **and Echinacea:** slightly raised planting prevents crowns rotting on heavier soils.

Follow-up Care

An important job to remember is staking, especially for taller plants, and this is best carried out as soon as plants emerge in spring. That way the structures are camouflaged by leaf growth. Some plants are slug and snail targets and early action prevents displays being ruined. *See* page 209.

Perennial Support

Don't wait for a sudden downpour to batter your delphiniums or flatten stately achillea! You can support your plants in several ways:

Top Tip

Cut back by about a third to a half in late spring (around the time of the Chelsea Flower Show hence the expression 'doing the Chelsea chop'). This delays flowering but makes plants bushier. This is an effective pruning time for many tall, late summer- and autumn-flowering perennials ('Herbstfreude').

▶ **Pea sticks:** Twiggy sticks often cut from hazel but any prunings will do.

▶ **Wire mesh:** Twist into a dome and hold in place with sticks. This is ideal for forcing sprawling plants like geraniums to grow upwards first.

▶ **Canes and twine:** Surround the clump with canes and tie in twine network.

▶ **Ready-made frames and support solutions:** Simply push in or link together.

Growing Bulbs

Bulbs are one of the most versatile plant groups and can provide years of seasonal colour and enjoyment for very little care. Hardy spring-, summer- and autumn-flowering bulbs as well as tender summer-flowering corms and tubers like gladioli and dahlias, are all classed as perennials. Spring bulbs, as well as a few autumn-flowering bulbs and early summer-flowering ornamental alliums, appear in the shops in late summer and with the exception of tulips should be planted as soon as possible. Summer-flowering types including lilies, are typically available early to mid spring.

Buying Bulbs

Though it is cheaper to buy dry bulbs, many spring-flowering types are now available for instant effect,

potted up and ready to flower. Just remove the pot and plant without disturbing the bulbs. Dry bulbs can deteriorate rapidly in warm conditions so check packets carefully avoiding any with the following symptoms:

▶ Shrivelled or pitted surface

▶ Soft when squeezed gently

▶ Excessive blue mould on surface

▶ Missing outer skin, especially with tulips

▶ Already sprouting (crocus bulbs are an exception)

Planting Bulbs

The general rule for planting is to make the hole 2 1/2 times the depth of the bulb. If you plant bulbs at the wrong depth they can move to the correct level themselves, but this uses up reserves, so it's best to get it right first time. Follow instructions on the packet allowing space for bulbs to multiply if naturalizing or planting for long-term displays. Daffodils and other bulbs can stop flowering when cramped. Save time and

Top Tip

Tulips are notorious for not flowering as well in their second year. For reliable blooming in well-drained borders, plant 23 cm (9 in) deep and go for easy-to-please single late types, Darwin hybrid and Triumph groups.

energy by digging holes to accommodate several bulbs at a time in swathes or clusters. Check preferred soil type and light levels and if naturalizing in woodland for example, pick shade-tolerant bulbs (*see* page 127).

Planting in the Green

Some bulbs do not establish as well from dry bulbs as they do from clumps dug up straight after flowering. If possible plant snowdrops (*Galanthus*), English bluebells (*Hyacinthoides non-scripta*) and winter aconite (*Eranthis hyemalis*) 'in the green'.

How to Plant Bedding

Pansies flower year round. Plant in autumn for winter/spring flowering

Grow on seedlings bought from the garden centre

Half-hardy annuals like petunia, busy Lizzie and French marigold are the kinds of plants that traditionally come under the term summer bedding. There are winter and spring bedding plants too (planted in autumn) including violas and pansies, double daisies, primroses and polyanthus, forget-me-nots and wallflowers. But summer bedding also now includes a wide range of tender perennials, sometimes called patio plants, which tend to bloom over a much longer period. Traditional bedding fuchsias and geraniums (*Pelargonium*) are today joined by diascia, nemesia and trailing verbena, which do just as well in borders as in baskets and containers.

87

Trays and Pots

Half-hardy annuals tend to appear in garden centres long before the last likely frost is due so if you buy at this time, you must keep plants frost free until it is safe to plant out. Seed-raised plants usually come in divided trays, while tender perennials produced from cuttings are typically sold in individual pots. To save money you can also buy seedlings and plantlets/plug plants in early spring, to prick out or pot on at home on a warm window ledge or heated greenhouse.

Planting

After thorough watering, carefully remove from packaging trays or pots, holding plants by their roots. Use a trowel to make a hole in prepared and improved soil. As you plant, ensure that the rootball is completely covered but none of the lower leaves or stems are buried. Firm lightly with the flat of your hands and water-in steadily, avoiding disturbing the soil. Allow sufficient room between individual plants for them to fill out. To encourage bushiness, pinch out the tips of snapdragons (*Antirrhinum*) and red bedding salvias if this hasn't already been done.

Boosting Mixed Borders

Although traditional summer-bedding displays often had their own designated areas and were replaced at the end of the season with bulbs and spring-flowering bedding, nowadays tender perennials and half-hardy annuals are used to add extra colour in mixed borders. The planting is more natural and gap filling works particularly well with plants that look more like herbaceous perennials such as cosmos and diascia. *See* page 192 for more ideas.

Checklist

▶ **Planting:** Improve ground prior to planting using bulky organic matter or fertilizer. Buy and plant bare-root trees, roses and hedging in dormant periods.

▶ **Trees:** Plant trees in a generous hole, spreading bare roots. Protect tree bark from rabbits and squirrels. Use mulch or tree mats to cut competition from weeds.

▶ **Shrubs:** Plant most container-grown shrubs and climbers avoiding frost and drought.

▶ **Herbs:** Plant Mediterranean herbs, tender shrubs and evergreens mid spring.

▶ **Alpines:** Plant low-maintenance herb and alpine beds through membrane with gravel mulch.

▶ **Water matters:** Increase drainage prior to planting herbs, silver-leaved plants and alpines. Create a shallow depression around woody plants to allow water to soak in where needed.

▶ **Shelter:** Erect windbreak around evergreens and conifers in exposed sites.

▶ **Support:** Stake trees and larger 'specimen'-sized shrubs to prevent wind-rock. Plant climbers and wall shrubs at least 45 cm (18 in) from wall and provide support.

▶ **Perennials:** Plant herbaceous and other perennials at recommended planting distances. Support taller perennials.

▶ **Bulbs:** Plant bulbs at the correct depth and space well if naturalizing. Plant hard to establish bulbs 'in the green'.

▶ **Gaps:** Fill border gaps with half-hardy annuals and tender perennials.

Planning Your Borders

Border Design

The design of beds and borders partly depends on the overall layout and size of your plot and the shape and position of the buildings and features in it. Borders can unite different elements and create a pleasing flow from one area to the next, or even direct the eye to a particular spot.

Measuring Up and Laying Out

Ideally, make a scale drawing of the garden, or a smaller area within it, using graph paper. This allows you to see the space clearly and work out how to arrange the beds and borders so that they relate well to other features such as a patio, lawn, pool or a

Mark a circle or arc using string to measure the radius

new conservatory. Use a hosepipe or length of rope to experiment with different shapes and sizes. View from various angles including upstairs and tweak accordingly. Represent specimen trees, large shrubs etc. with bamboo canes for a rough 3D impression.

Mark and Cut Edges

Transfer the shapes and measurements from your plan to the ground by pushing in tent pegs at intervals or driving in wooden pegs. Connect with high visibility twine. To make cutting easier, use a spray can of white, line-marker paint, then remove the pegs and string and cut to shape. If you have a lot of lawn to remove, hire a turf-cutting machine.

Top Tip

To keep borders running along garden boundaries in scale with the walls, fences and hedges, extend them in places so that they are as deep as the screen is high. Once the newly planted border starts to grow, especially where schemes include blocks of taller shrubs and perennials, they will look perfectly proportioned.

Quick Border Upgrade

Existing borders can be improved in a number of ways:

▶ **Edges:** Smooth out wiggly-edged beds using broad sweeping curves.

▶ **Width:** Widen narrow, tram-line borders to make more space for creative planting.

▶ **Depth:** Vary the depth of borders down the garden to create hidden aspects. A broad s-shape is easy to superimpose on a rectangular lawn.

▶ **Round off:** Replace a squared-off corner bed with a long, smooth arc for a more dynamic and contemporary touch.

Shapes and Sizes

The scale and design of beds and borders can have a big influence on the feel of your garden. Changing the shape and size of existing beds is one of the easiest ways to update your garden and give it a completely new look. Be bold and dynamic when tackling a garden with borders that slavishly follow the boundaries, and also be as generous as possible in the amount of space given over to plants. Lawns and paved areas can often dominate gardens.

Extend borders in places to keep them in scale with walls and fences

93

Gap Fillers

In a strip between wall and paving, where soil is not very deep, you need tough plants with running roots or a self-seeding habit to colonize.

Hypericum

Try planting:

▶ *Alchemilla mollis* (lady's mantle)
▶ *Anemone x hybrida*
   (Japanese anemone)
▶ *Campanula poscharskyana* 'Stella' (trailing bellflower)
▶ *Euphorbia amygdaloides* var. *robbiae* (wood spurge)
▶ *Geranium cantabrigiense* 'Cambridge' (cranesbill)
▶ *Geranium macrorrhizum* 'Ingwersen's Variety' (cranesbill)
▶ *Hedera helix* 'Little Diamond' (English ivy)
▶ *Hypericum calycinum* (rose of Sharon)
▶ *Origanum vulgare* 'Aureum' (golden marjoram)
▶ *Vinca* (periwinkle – greater and lesser)

Narrow Strips

These borders are not ideal as plant selection is limited and you have fewer opportunities for creative combinations. Strips between a wall or fence and between paving or tarmac are especially difficult, as they tend to be dry with little soil depth. But adding a border here helps soften hard lines and makes it possible to hide dividing structures with climbers and wall shrubs. One way to introduce more variety and create the

Informal planting helps to blend the garden with the wild landscape beyond the boundary

illusion of depth is to plant in long, thin overlapping bands rather than the usual rounded blocks. Punctuate with the occasional taller specimen such as the graceful ornamental grass *Stipa gigantea*.

Deep Borders

With more space you can combine a much wider range of plants sizes and types. Deeper borders with lush planting help camouflage boundaries and in small gardens this gives the illusion of space. Running wide borders around a circular or oval lawn is especially effective in a tiny plot. The only downside to deep borders is access so set a discreet line of stepping stones through for maintenance.

Organic Shapes

Go for broad curves and flowing lines for a sense of relaxation. Organic shapes contrast strikingly with crisp contemporary architecture. They accommodate uneven ground and help to create seamless links between different elements within a garden. These carefree shapes also tie in well with a surrounding rural landscape if parts of your garden look out onto countryside. Consider a narrow, elongated s-shaped or snaking lawn with borders around it if you have a long narrow garden. It will create an air of mystery with parts waiting to be explored around each corner.

Formal Figures

Crisp-edged beds and borders, with a geometric ground plan, work particularly well with period properties or architectural pastiches of Tudor or Georgian buildings. The border shapes can be emphasized and plants such as shrub roses and perennials within the beds 'contained' by a low hedge of clipped box. Formality can also suit modern buildings: for a soft contemporary look try blocks of naturalistic grasses and perennials within paving.

95

Island Beds

Walk-round borders used to be all the rage in the 1970s but they still have a place in our gardens today. Planting is slightly tricky though as it needs to look good viewed from all angles. Typically island beds are informal in design with broad grassy pathways providing access and they tend to suit larger rural gardens.

Raised Beds

Though originally designed to give herbs, vegetables and alpines better drainage or deeper soil, adding raised beds filled with ornamental plants is a great way to vary height in a totally flat site or within a paved garden. They lift plants to a convenient height for maintenance and can also double as impromptu seating. Construction materials include:

▶ **Wooden sleepers:** A convenient construction material with a contemporary feel.

▶ **Brick:** One of the more expensive options but, depending on whether you use reclaimed or tumbled bricks to create the illusion of age, or new bricks, it can suit period gardens or modern landscapes.

▶ **Stone:** Commonly used to create beds for alpines but rough stone also looks good with cottage garden flowers.

▶ **Rendered blockwork:** This relatively inexpensive construction method can be tailored to any garden style you desire.

96

Backdrops

A simple backdrop provides a foil for plants, helping to show flowers and foliage to best effect. Walls, fences, trellis panels and hedges have different characteristics, varying the overall look of the garden. Man-made backdrops have the advantage of being able to support climbers and wall shrubs. Hedges, though they require regular maintenance, have many plus points and when fully grown, usually work out much cheaper than man-made structures of an equivalent height.

Wooden Structures

Fencing and trellis panels, hazel hurdles or brushwood screens are quick to erect and relatively inexpensive. They take up very little room and, with tanalised or concrete posts, basic fencing and trellis should last at least ten years before repairs are needed.

Fences
Panels vary in design and durability. Provided they are raised off the soil or have replaceable gravel boards along the base, they shouldn't rot. If you have inherited mismatched fence panels or just want to upgrade your fence, try the following:

▶ Use a heavy-duty staple gun to attach heather, brushwood, willow or bamboo screen roll to disguise ugly panels.

97

▶ Add finials to posts for a smart, period look.

▶ Paint or stain mismatched fence panels to create a uniform backdrop.

▶ Apply paint or stain to strengthen a colour scheme or provide a striking contrast e.g. a blue backdrop for a hot orange and red border.

Screens and Hurdles

Woven hazel or willow hurdles have the ideal rustic look for a cottage or country border. Try combining with a new hedge. The latter should be established by the time the hurdles disintegrate. Paint with matt yacht varnish to extend life. Fix hurdles to angle irons with black electrical cable ties and screw screen panels to wooden posts.

Trellis

Top solid fence panels with trellis to let in more light and provide support for climbers. Use full- sized trellis panels to create see-through walls around interior garden rooms. Trellis comes in basic square or diamond patterns as well as more intricate designs. Try attaching shaped trellis panels to battens to brighten up a dull wall.

Top Tip

The rain shadow effect makes the strip of ground at the base of a wall or fence constantly dry. An added problem is protruding wall footings, or buried rubble and concrete. Dig out as much loose material as you can and add bulky organic matter (manure or garden compost) to counter the effect.

Walls

Brick or stone walls are expensive but do add character and a feeling of permanence. Build cheaper alternatives using rendered breeze blocks. Rendering hides a multitude of sins including mismatched brick and stone, but the uniform backdrop is ideal for flower borders. A white painted wall might give the garden a Mediterranean look while a vibrantly painted wall can add a contemporary twist.

Traditional Materials

Tall boundaries of weathered or reclaimed brick create the look of a Victorian or Edwardian walled garden. Modern brickwork can look stark unless it is softened by climbers, wall shrubs or trellis. Rough or drystone walls suit country gardens and naturalistic planting, while taller boundaries of dressed stone, typical of period properties, suggest formality and a touch of grandeur.

Hedges

A smooth, trimmed hedge of yew, beech, holly or western red cedar acts like green architecture whilst mixed and wildlife hedges are inevitably less formal looking. Whatever hedge you plan, note eventual height and spread as well as maintenance needs and leave a pathway at the back of the border to allow access for cutting. Hedges draw moisture and nutrients from the ground around them so adjacent plants need extra help to thrive.

Hedge Benefits

A well cared for hedge is a long lasting asset in the garden and has several key benefits:

▶ Evergreen hedges or beech (with coppery leaves through winter) add year-round colour.

▶ Living boundaries attract wildlife by providing food, shelter and nesting places for birds.

▶ In exposed gardens, taller hedges can act as windbreakers.

Hedges for Wildlife

A mixed 'country' hedge creates an ideal habitat for wildlife. Include the following, using hawthorn (Crataegus monogyna) or blackthorn (Prunus spinosa) as the backbone:

▶ *Acer campestre* (field maple)
▶ *Cornus sanguinea* (common dogwood)
▶ *Coryllus avellana* (hazel)
▶ *Euonymus europaeus* (spindle tree)
▶ *Ilex aquifolium* (holly)
▶ *Rosa canina* (dog rose)
▶ *Sambucus nigra* (elder)
▶ *Viburnum opulus* (guelder rose)
▶ *Viburnum lantana* (wayfaring tree)

Designing with Plants

Plants are the wall colourings and soft furnishings that bring outdoor rooms to life. The way in which you overlay the underlying footprint of the garden with flowers and foliage determines the whole atmosphere and appeal of the space. You don't have to have an artistic bent as there are guidelines regarding colour, shape, textural contrast and seasonality that can help you to put plants together in an inspiring and visually rewarding way.

Varying Height

It is important to stage plants effectively to make the most of their individual attributes as well as how they support one another as a group. In the first place you need to know how tall and wide they are likely to get. A big solid plant placed too far forward will obscure plants behind and the reverse is true with dainty little specimens which need to be at the front where you can appreciate them.

Arranging by Height

No matter how small your borders are, it is essential to work in some height variation. But avoid being overly regimented as this can give lacklustre results even with a bright colour scheme. Bringing some taller groupings forward in undulating waves works well in long, deep beds.

Dahlias

▶ **Front:** Carpeting and mound-forming alpines, herbs and ground cover plants; dwarf bulbs; short herbaceous and evergreen perennials; grasses and sedges; low-growing shrubs; patio and miniature roses. Summer additions include half-hardy annual bedding; tender perennial patio plants.

▶ **Middle:** Most herbaceous plants; taller hardy and half-hardy annuals; tender perennials e.g. fuchsias and summer-flowering bulbs and tubers like dahlias. Try bush (hybrid tea and floribunda) and shorter-growing shrub roses; medium-growing flowering and foliage shrubs.

▶ **Back:** Small ornamental trees; taller grasses and herbaceous perennials; many evergreen and deciduous shrubs; columnar bamboos.

Textural Contrast

It is useful to try to visualize plants in black and white as too much emphasis on colour can overshadow the importance of varying plant shapes and textures. Remember that when a plant is not in bloom, its foliage is likely to be the key feature so having two or three plants together with a similar leaf shape or the same overall form is not ideal.

Top Tip
The trick to keeping borders interesting is unpredictability. Mix things up by dotting the occasional tall plant further forward. Try 'see-through' specimens like *Verbena bonariensis* and bronze fennel or an airy ornamental grass such as *Molinia caerulea arundinacea*.

Flower Shapes

▶ **Ball:** *Allium, Echinops*, dahlia (some), *Viburnum opulus* 'Roseum'

▶ **Dome:** *Agapanthus, Angelica, Clerodendron bungei, Hydrangea* 'Annabelle'

▶ **Spike:** *Actaea*, lavender, *Perovskia, Veronicastrum*

▶ **Column:** delphinium, lupin, *Verbascum*

▶ **Cone:** *Buddleja, Hydrangea paniculata, Lysimachia clethroides*

▶ **Bowl:** *Anemone x hybrida*, peony, poppy, *Rhomnea*, rose

▶ **Trumpet:** lily, *Crinodendron*, daffodil, hosta

▶ **Daisy:** *Anthemis, Coreopsis, Cosmos, Echinacea, Leucanthemum, Rudbeckia*

▶ **Cloud:** *Alchemilla mollis, Crambe cordifolia, Deschampsia, Gypsophila, Thalictrum, Stipa*

▶ **Plate:** *Achillea*, fennel, lace-cap hydrangeas, *Verbena*

▶ **Tubular:** *Cuphea*, some fuchsia, *Phygellius*

▶ **Bell:** *Campanula*, some clematis, foxglove, *Penstemon, Platycodon*

Foliage Shapes

▶ **Linear:** *Crocosmia*, many grasses and sedges *(Carex); Iris sibirica*, dwarf *Kniphofia*

▶ **Sword/strap-shaped:** *Astelia, Iris* (many), *Phormium*, yucca

▶ **Rounded:** *Astilboides tabularis, Bergenia, Darmera*

▶ **Heart-shaped:** *Brunnera, Epimedium*, hosta, some rhododendron

▶ **Lobed:** *Anemone x hybrida*, geranium, *Sidalcea*

▶ **Jaggedly divided:** *Acanthus spinosus*, cardoon, *Rheum palmatum*

▶ **Pinnate:** *Gleditsia, Polemonium, Sorbus, Wisteria*

▶ **Palmate:** hellebore, lupin, *Rodgersia aesculifolia*

▶ **Feathery:** *Astilbe, Dicentra*, fennel, most ferns

103

Viburnum opulus
(Japanese snowball)

Head and Tails

Breaking down the shapes and textures of plants, looking at flower and foliage separately, allows you to mix and match more effectively. *See* page 103 for examples of some of the shapes you could play around with. For example, you might set a plant with ball-shaped blooms next to a daisy-flowered specimen or one with large, rounded leaves next to one with sword-shaped blades.

Contrasting Plants

Some plants have a distinctly upright or vertical feel e.g. ones with linear foliage including many grasses; plants with strongly upright and parallel stems e.g. the bamboo *Phyllostachys nigra*, or parallel flower spikes e.g. *Veronicastrum* and *Iris sibirica*. Low-growing shrubs with tiered foliage such as junipers or with layers of flowers e.g. *Viburnum plicatum*; or herbaceous plants where the flat flower heads are all held in the same plane e.g. *Achillea*, feel horizontal in character. Try contrasting these forms, emphasizing the difference by setting taller upright plants next to shorter, horizontal or spreading plants.

Planting Techniques

In very small mixed borders you are quite likely to be planting singly or for small plants including summer bedding, in groups of three or five (even numbers are very hard to place naturally – like trying to arrange four daffodils in a vase). For deeper or longer beds there are more creative options for combining flowers and foliage and you might want to use different

Top Tip

Remember that one shrub, a columnar bamboo, a large ornamental grass or sculptural perennial like cardoon, can effectively be counted as a block.

approaches depending where in the garden the border is situated. For example, a naturalistic display would work well around a large pond, beneath a group of trees or along the garden's furthest margins.

Blocks

The more of a single variety you can group together the greater the impact will be. And for daintier annuals and perennials as well as bulbs, having them massed in the border is often the best way to appreciate them. Block sizes depend on the scale of the border. For example, to make more of the lacquer-red winter stems of dogwood in a winter border, you might plant five or more shrubs whereas in a smaller bed you might only have room for one. Though blocks of plants are typically represented on paper plans as broadly oval shapes, groups can fit together like pieces of a jigsaw and have uneven margins. Once differently sized blocks start to grow and knit together with their neighbours, the original layout shapes are softened.

Drifts

Planting bulbs, annuals, perennials and ornamental grasses in drifts creates a more naturalistic feel and allows you to mingle a single variety with more of its neighbours to great effect. Drifts of relatively tall and airy plants can be narrow and sinuous, weaving their way through other plants and perhaps even lazily meandering diagonally across the bed from front to back. You can also make broader drifts through neighbouring blocks to create the impression of movement in an otherwise static layout.

Mosaics

The meadow or prairie style of planting that is currently very much in vogue looks to nature for inspiration. In the wild, areas are often colonized by a group or matrix of plants that appears to be mixed in reasonably stable proportions. Within this background one of the plants might suddenly become more prolific. Think of a cornfield with streaks of red poppies or a grassy meadow where buttercups create drifts of intense yellow in one or two areas. Other plants also pop up within the mosaic of flower and foliage, adding dots of colour and textural contrast. The whole effect has been likened to the pointillist method of painting – combining plants really is another art form!

Ground Cover Tapestry

It is okay to keep plants forming a carpet at the same low level if there are taller shrubs, bamboos or trees rising out of the ground cover that can provide suitable height contrast. Plant a tapestry effect by interweaving creeping carpeters and bulbs.

Exclamation Marks

Certain tall, narrow, strikingly upright plants or ones with a bold spiky outline can really draw the eye. Use them to punctuate a border, marking key points such as the end of a bed, a change in level, or the threshold between one area and another. Conifers or shrubs with a rigid form, especially evergreens, can also be spaced regularly to set up a visual rhythm along the length of a formal border. Living exclamation marks include:

Berberis thunbergii
'Helmond Pillar'

106

Top Tip

Don't rely too heavily on flowers
for creating colour schemes.
Foliage is more enduring and
coloured-leaf and variegated-
foliage plants provide
a surprisingly wide palette.

▶ *Berberis thunbergii* 'Helmond Pillar'

▶ *Calamagrostis x acutiflora* 'Stricta' (feather reed grass)

▶ *Cordyline australis* (cabbage palm)

▶ *Cupressus sempervirens* 'Stricta' (Italian cypress)

▶ *Juniperus scopulorum* 'Blue Arrow'

▶ *Phormium tenax* cultivars (New Zealand flax)

▶ *Taxus baccata* 'Standishii' (golden fastigiate yew)

▶ *Yucca flaccida* 'Gold Sword'

Making a Planting Plan

Even a rough outline of what plant or plant grouping goes where will help you iron out the kinks in your design. Ideally, make a scale drawing of the border and sketch in the various elements, taking into account planting distance and height as well as colour and period of interest. Transfer these positions to the bed using an array of bamboo canes, small, medium and large containers/used plastic plant pots, as stand-ins for trees, shrubs and perennials.

Colour Scheming

In the summer garden many shades overlay the green backdrop. The most vibrant come from flowers, though in spring and autumn certain shrubs and trees can rival their display. Fruits and berries, tree bark and the stems of shrubs like dogwood and willow also contribute to the spectrum of living colour.

The Colour Wheel

One of the most useful devices in being able to successfully combine shades in planting schemes is the artist's colour wheel. This shows the primary colours of yellow, blue and red and the blended results in between. Broadly speaking you are 'safe' working with a group of adjacent colours such as yellow, orange and scarlet or blue, purple and cerise. For a more dynamic feel, go to the opposite colour on the wheel and add these contrasting shades as highlights.

Dramatic Highlights

You don't have to rely solely on plant colours when designing a scheme. In a border of orange and yellow blooms for example you might use a blue painted wooden obelisk as a focal point, the effect intensified by the use of a colour on the opposite side of the wheel. And in a bed of rhododendron you could enliven the solid green backdrop that remains after flowering, using an eye-catching lacquer-red glazed jar. Paired, 'opposing' colours create a bright, fresh look. Try lemon yellow with touches of violet purple, or lime-green foliage and day-glow pink or cerise blooms.

Shades of Harmony

Pastels have always been popular for flower borders but to avoid these schemes looking insipid, some colours should be represented as darker or more intense shades. For example, in a cottage scheme of soft blues, pinks and purples, you could include some deeper crimson roses, dark-blue delphiniums or purple clematis. And in a prairie style scheme of grasses mingled with a variety of yellow and orange daisy flowers, include some rust, bronze and mahogany shades.

Nature's Shades

You will find more of the shades you're looking for amongst plants at certain times of the year as there are natural cycles of colour.

▶ **Spring:** There is an abundance of bright lime-green foliage, and white, yellow and blue flowers, so avoid trying to create a hot scheme early in the year.

▶ **Summer:** The full spectrum is available including many vibrant and eye-catching shades like scarlet and orange which are largely absent from the spring palette.

▶ **Autumn:** Leaf colours are golden or fiery, the shades frequently reflected in late- flowering herbaceous and tender perennials, but there are also purples and blues, which allow for rich contrasts.

▶ **Winter:** Apart from coloured stems, fruits and evergreen foliage, the natural landscape is muted.

A Riot of Colour

Enjoyment of colour is a question of personal taste. There's nothing to stop you rejecting the 'rules' of colour scheming and making your borders a blooming kaleidoscope; there are no colour clashes in nature. However some colour groupings can affect the atmosphere within sections of a garden, so if you want to make an area feel lively, energetic and stimulating, perhaps around an al fresco dining and entertaining spot, go for a hot, zingy scheme. Meanwhile if you want to create a calm and restful environment consider cool, soothing hues.

109

These cool colours create a calming atmosphere

▶ **Hot:** Combine flowers in scarlet, orange, golden yellow, coral pink, violet and cerise with purple and bronze tinted leaves.

▶ **Cool:** Focus on blue, purple, cool blue-pinks, lemon yellow and white blooms, and add silver, lime green and white variegated foliage.

Monochrome Borders

The most difficult schemes to pull off are single colour or monochrome types, but when they work they can be incredibly beautiful and striking. Famous examples in Britain are Sissinghurst Castle's white garden in Kent and the red borders at Hidcote Manor, Gloucestershire. The key is including subtle shades of the chosen hue and backing the blooms up with appropriately coloured foliage. For example in a red border you could include the light scarlet-reds of poppies through to the black-reds of certain dahlias. And for foliage, include plenty of green (red is opposite on the colour wheel) as well as red-tinged, bronze and purple-red foliage.

Modulating Colour

Colour can be varied within a border, in places building up visual excitement to reach a dramatic and eye-popping crescendo before subsiding into a cooler more tranquil section. The effect can be likened to the varied movements of a symphony.

Manipulating Perspective

Some colours foreshorten the view whilst others make areas feel more distant – think of the blues, purples and greys of distant hills. Combine advancing and retreating colours to alter perspective.

▶ **Advancing:** Keep eye-catching white, yellow or bright red closer to the house and avoid at the end of a border, pathway or garden.

▶ **Retreating:** Use blues, purples, greys and silvers in the further reaches to make the plot feel even longer.

Make an all blue border work by adding touches of purple and gold

111

Cosmos 'White Sonata'

Plant a Moon Garden

Pale flower and foliage colours stand out at night, especially when the moon is out. Several have a heady evening fragrance designed to attract moth pollinators but these plants also create a wonderful environment around a subtly lit sitting area. Try the following, which are scented or keep open at night, along with silver-leaved foliage plants like cardoon, artemisia and lamb's ear (*Stachys byzantina*) or white-variegated *Cornus alba* 'Elegantissima'.

▶ *Cosmos* 'White Sonata' (cosmos)
▶ *Hesperis matronalis* (Dame's violet)
▶ *Jasminum officinale* (jasmine)
▶ *Lilium longiflorum* (Easter lily)
▶ *Lonicera pericymenum* (honeysuckle)
▶ *Lychnis coronaria* 'Alba' (white flowered dusty miller)
▶ *Matthiola bicornis* (night-scented stock)
▶ *Nicotiana sylvestris* (woodland tobacco)
▶ *Oenothera biennis* (evening primrose)
▶ *Philadelphus* (mock orange)
▶ *Phlox paniculata* 'Alba Grandiflora' (border phlox)

Did You Know?

The blue, yellow and white colours of wild spring blooms are designed to attract early pollinating insects like flies and bees. Vibrant summer flowers draw butterflies and bees alike, while some of our red- coloured garden varieties are pollinated by birds in their native country e.g. fuchsias from South America are hummingbird favourites and the Australian bottle brushes (*Callistemon*) are visited by members of the parrot family. In winter, there are so few insects that plants often use powerful fragrance rather than showy blooms to attract them.

Philadelphus (mock orange)

Planning Seasonal Highlights

In small gardens there's not usually room to successfully divide planted areas into separate spring, summer, autumn and winter beds but you can focus on certain areas at different times of year by grouping plants that come to prominence.

This Season's Collection

Much like in a fashion show, you can put together a group of subjects that work well together and really make a statement. Look at the following for inspiration:

▶ **Spring:** Beneath trees, white-variegated, blue-flowered *Brunnera macrophylla* 'Jack Frost', white-flowered *Helleborus x hybridus*, yellow and white cyclamineus daffodil 'February Silver', blue dwarf bulb *Scilla sibirica* and purple carpeting *Ajuga* 'Catlin's Giant'.

▶ **Summer:** *Clematis* Perle d'Azur with the apricot English rose 'Sweet Juliet', tall spires of *Verbascum* 'Helen Johnson', lime-green flowered annual tobacco plant (*Nicotiana*) and English lavender (*Lavandula* 'Hidcote').

Delphiniums and day lilies

113

▶ **Autumn:** Berry backdrop of *Pyracantha* Orange Glow, fiery *Nandina domestica* leaves, purple-blue Michaelmas daisy (e.g. *Aster x frikartii* 'Monch') and the bulb, *Colchicum speciosum* 'Album'.

▶ **Winter:** Scarlet-stemmed *Cornus alba* 'Sibirica', glossy mahogany leaves of *Bergenia cordifolia* 'Purpurea', white-flowered heather *Erica x darleyensis* 'Silbersmelze' and double snowdrops.

Locating Seasonal Beds

Think of where you spend most of your time in the garden as the year progresses. If you have a greenhouse or potting shed, you might want to concentrate spring interest plantings around them and

Pyracantha

along the route from the house. In summer you probably spend more time out in the garden as a whole, not just the patio, and perhaps planting for summer interest could be focused around a lawn where children play, a summer house or arbour. Autumn colour could be set beneath existing trees or shrubs with fiery tints or autumn fruits and, for winter enjoyment, make a sparkling collection that's easily viewed from the house.

Dual-season Plants

Particularly in smaller gardens, pick plants that have more than one season of interest e.g. a crab apple (*Malus* 'Evereste') which has spring blossom and colourful autumn fruits or the white-variegated dogwood, *Cornus alba* 'Elegantissima' whose cherry red winter stems are an extra bonus. Always consider the ornamental value of the foliage of herbaceous perennials before buying.

Year Round Borders

If you are planting or revamping a mixed border of shrubs and perennials, a little forward planning can go a long way towards creating a display that has interest and beauty through the year.

Essential Ingredients

Arrange a core planting of a small ornamental tree, preferably with more than one season of interest; a late summer flowering deciduous

Crab apples

115

Purple cone flowers (*Echinacea*) bloom over a long period

shrub like hydrangea, with a winter presence, and at least one evergreen shrub chosen for its colourful foliage through the year. Add the following as space allows:

▶ **Drought-busters:** Evergreen-flowering and foliage-interest herbs and alpines including lavender, Russian sage (*Perovskia atriplicifolia* 'Blue Spire') and rock rose (*Helianthemum*) that will keep performing even in a summer drought.

▶ **Long-flowering perennials:** Long-flowering herbaceous perennials – spring, summer and autumn focus – with attractive foliage.

▶ **Evergreen perennials:** Colourful evergreen perennials such as *Heuchera* and *x Heucherella*.

▶ Repeat flowering: A climber that flowers for several months (e.g. *Viticella* hybrid clematis).

Perovskia atriplicifolia (Russian sage)

▶ **Bulbs:** Bulb collection with varieties chosen to flower from early winter, through spring to early summer.

▶ **Seasonal plants:** Annuals that respond well to dead-heading and long-flowered tender perennials (fuchsia, dahlia, diascia).

116

Checklist

▶ **First steps:** Measure and draw up basic border shapes.

▶ **Beds:** Cut out new beds from lawned areas and upgrade existing borders by reshaping and widening. Plant very narrow beds with tough ground cover, wall shrubs and climbers.

▶ **Maximize space:** Create deep borders to camouflage boundaries in small gardens.

▶ **Mirror landscape:** Select free-flowing or formal border designs depending on garden's architecture and surrounding landscape. Increase interest in a flat site using raised beds.

▶ **Backdrop:** Create a suitable backdrop to show planting to best advantage.

▶ **Hedges:** Consider planting a hedge to benefit wildlife or to grow a more substantial divide than you could afford to build.

▶ **Staggered height:** Arrange border plants roughly by height but break the rules occasionally e.g. with taller see-through plants.

▶ **Variety:** Contrast habit, flower and foliage shapes and textures. Consider different planting styles e.g. drifts and mosaics.

▶ **Add drama:** Use plants with a bold outline as exclamation marks. Refer to an artist's colour wheel to work out schemes. Use colour to create dynamic peaks and troughs along a border, to manipulate perspective or create an ambience.

▶ **Constant colour:** Plan seasonal border highlights using appropriate plant groupings. Include plants for year-round enjoyment including bulbs, evergreens and annuals.

Right Plant, Right Place

Local Inspiration

Look in other people's gardens for landscaping ideas and attractive plant combinations. See if you can narrow down what grows well in your area and if there are plant types suited to the locale. For example in a coastal area you could see quite a lot of pines, succulents, grasses and shrubs like hebe and hydrangea, as well as silver and grey leaf herbs and alpines. Speak to local experts about the climate and how best to tackle soil conditions and consider joining a gardening club which offers support for beginners.

Gathering Information

Whether you take over an existing garden or are developing a new plot, the look of the soil and the way plants are growing can tell you quite a lot about the condition of the ground. There is no guarantee that previous occupants took notice of soil pH or drainage problems. If you discover an ailing rhododendron, for example, and everything else seems healthy there is a good chance that the soil is alkaline. Dig a few holes and carry out a pH test to verify any suspicions. Also note the direction of prevailing winds and any microclimate anomalies such as frost pockets (*see* page 23).

Hebe grows well in coastal areas

Visiting Parks and Gardens

Pop into local centres throughout the year and try to attend a few courses run by staff at horticultural colleges and botanic gardens. You will discover what might grow well in your garden as well as how to deal with any growing problems or challenges. Sites open to the public often have labelled specimens

so take a notebook with you. Jot down individual trees, shrubs or plant groupings
that you particularly like the look of and that are in scale with your plot.

Other Sources

Places to look for information specific to your planting area include:

▶ Garden centres and local specialist plant nurseries
▶ Private gardens open for visitors
▶ Conservation centres (to see what the original wild vegetation was like)
▶ Libraries
▶ Internet sites and blogs

Dry and Sunny

Most of the aromatic culinary herbs can survive in a hot, dry environment, as can many alpines and succulent ground cover plants. What they tend to have in common is a waxy or leathery coating or a covering of light reflecting hairs, wool or white powder – all designed to slow moisture loss from the plant. Leaves and stems might also be thick and fleshy, storing moisture to tide them over dry spells. Many have a reduced leaf area and others might even have shed conventional leaves altogether like most cacti.

Hot Beds

South- or west-facing borders of free-draining soil, especially those backed by a wall, fence or hedge, could get very dry indeed and, without irrigation, only drought tolerant sun-lovers that enjoy a good

baking, would thrive. The situation can be worse in narrow beds next to the house where rainwater may not reach the ground. In order to conserve water, it's important to use plants that will thrive here.

Drought-resistant Shrubs and Climbers

The following plants thrive in a well-drained sunny border, for example on gravelly soils. Consider mulching with gravel or stone chippings to set off the silver and grey foliage and to conserve moisture.

- *Abelia x grandiflora*
- *Buddleja davidii* (butterfly bush)
- *Ceanothus* (Californian lilac)
- *Cistus* (rock rose)
- *Convolvulus cneorum*
- *Elaeagnus* 'Quicksilver'
- *Lavandula* (lavender)
- *Phlomis fruiticosa* (Jerusalem sage)
- *Rosmarinus officinalis* (rosemary)
- *Solanum crispum* 'Glasnevin' (potato vine)

Sempervivum (house leek)

Drought-resistant Perennials

These perennials and bulbs would work well together in a narrow border at the base of a wall or in a raised bed. Or, mix with the shrubs above to landscape larger beds. Once established, they will rarely need watering.

- *Agastache* (anise hyssop)
- *Allium* (ornamental onion)
- *Artemisia* 'Powis Castle'
- *Carex testacea* (leatherleaf sedge)
- *Centranthus ruber* and white form 'Albus' (red valerian)
- *Crocus*
- *Gaura lindheimeri*
- *Helictotrichon sempervirens* (blue oat grass)
- *Lychnis coronaria* (dusty miller)
- *Pennisetum alopecuroides*

- *Perovskia atriplicifolia* 'Blue Spire' (Russian sage)
- *Salvia x sylvestris* cultivars (ornamental sage)
- *Sedum* (e.g. 'Ruby Glow')
- *Sempervivum* (house leek)
- *Stipa gigantea* (Spanish oats)
- *Stipa tenuissima*
- *Styachys byzantina* (lamb's ear)
- *Teucrium hircanicum* 'Purple Tails'
- *Tulipa* (dwarf and species tulips)
- *Verbena bonariensis* (purple-top vervain)

123

Dry and Shady

One of the trickiest spots to plant a border is beneath overhanging trees. Not only is there shade to deal with but also the ground is frequently impoverished, dry and full of tree roots. But there are some useful strategies to improve growing conditions and a reasonable number of plants that will tough it out despite the less than ideal circumstances. Buildings can also create shade and coupled with the rain shadow effect, borders here may be dry though not nutrient poor.

Preparation and Planting

It's galling to see how well unwanted plants like brambles and wild-sown ivy do in dry shade beneath trees but at least it's an indication that some plants are adaptable. But even drought-tolerant types need a good start in life and some initial care while they establish a strong root system. Planting in autumn or late winter ensures reasonably moist ground.

Establishing Plants

Follow the advice below for creating a border that will thrive and need little ongoing maintenance:

Did You Know?

White variegation is
easier to maintain in
shade than yellow.

▶ Sprinkle a top dressing of general fertilizer such as fish,
blood and bone or pelleted chicken manure.

▶ Water the ground thoroughly and cover with
around 10 cm (4 in) of well-rotted manure or
garden compost.

▶ Plant through the mulch using young, vigorous plants where possible.

▶ Water in and keep mulch topped up.

Shrubs and Perennials for Dry Shade

The following are surprisingly tolerant of difficult terrain:

▶ *Dryopteris felix-mas* (male fern)
▶ *Epimedium* (barrenwort)
▶ *Euonymus fortunei* 'Emerald Gaiety'
▶ *Euphorbia amygdaloides var.robbiae*
(wood spurge)
▶ *Hedera helix* (English ivy) – plain or white-speckled
cultivars such as 'Green Ripple' or 'Glacier'
▶ *Geranium nodosum*
▶ *Helleborus foetidus* (stinking hellebore)
▶ *Iris foetidissima* and *I. f.* 'Variegata' (Gladwyn iris)
▶ *Lamium galeobdolon* (yellow archangel)
▶ *Mahonia aquifolium* (Oregon grape)

*Helleborus
foetidus
(stinking
hellebore)*

Woodland Effects

Planting conditions under trees are not always dry and impoverished. There is a wealth of desirable shrubs and pretty carpeting plants and bulbs to choose from if the soil is typically moisture-retentive from accumulated leaf litter. To achieve an atmospheric woodland scene, you only really need a single large specimen tree to begin with around which to build your border. Tree preservation orders often protect existing trees within new developments but you may also choose to plant two or three small trees to give the impression of a wild woodland glade.

Did You Know?

Because of the density of the leaf cover in summer, most woodland plants are late winter and spring blooming and may die back during summer because of the lack of light and moisture.

Woodland Understory

Beneath the tall tree canopy are layers of smaller trees and shade-tolerant shrubs. These are the understory plants that give natural woodland its tiered look. Try to emulate this in your border design. In addition, there are groundcover or woodland floor plants including herbaceous perennials, creepers, ferns and bulbs.

Pulmonaria

Shrubs and Perennials

Many woodland plants need acid soil (*see* pages 134–35 for ideas) but there are also lime-tolerant shrubs that thrive in shade including box (*Buxus sempervirens*), viburnum and bridal

126

wreath (*Spiraea arguta*) as well as perennials such as Bowles' golden grass (*Milium effusum* 'Aureum'), Japanese anemone (*Anemone x hybrida*) and hart's tongue fern (*Asplenium scolopendrium*). Try the following, along with the plants on pages 124–25 to build up the woodland look, mulching with well-rotted manure, leaf-mould or garden compost to retain moisture and the soil's organic content.

Understory Plants

▶ *Acer palmatum* (Japanese maple)
▶ *Hydrangea macrophylla* (mophead and lacecap hydrangeas)
▶ *Pieris*
▶ *Rhododendron luteum* and others (deciduous azalea)
▶ *Skimmia japonica* 'Rubella'

Groundcover

▶ *Brunnera macrophylla*
▶ *Digitalis purpurea* (foxglove)
▶ ferns (*see* page 57)
▶ *Geranium phaeum* 'Album'
▶ *Geranium sylvaticum* 'Album'
▶ *Helleborus x hybridus* (hellebore)
▶ *Lamium maculatum* 'White Nancy'
▶ *Pulmonaria*
▶ *x Heucherella* cultivars

Top Tip

Dig out a large planting hole for bigger shrubs, cutting out any crossing tree roots with secateurs or loppers. Back-fill with soil mixed with organic matter such as composted leaf mould.

Bulbs

▶ *Anemone nemorosa* (wood anemone), e.g. 'Robinsoniana'
▶ *Eranthis hyemalis* (winter aconite)
▶ *Galanthus* (snowdrop)
▶ hardy cyclamen
▶ *Narcissus* (cyclamineus daffodils)

127

Heavy Clay

This inherently fertile but badly drained soil can be converted into workable loam, but there's no getting over the fact that it might be a hard slog. In a dry summer, clay lacking in organic matter dries like concrete and as it shrinks, large cracks open up. Knowing when and how to cultivate clay is part of the challenge.

Gardening with Clay

Installing drainage pipes is expensive but some simple, low-tech changes can improve the situation sufficiently to grow a much wider range of plants. If you dig down far enough you will come to a layer of sticky orange clay below the darker topsoil. In waterlogged conditions, this subsoil layer will be grey due to the lack of oxygen – a useful warning sign that drainage needs improving. When cultivating borders, avoid bringing clay subsoil to the surface.

Ways to Improve Clay

▶ **Timing:** Don't work wet clay that sticks to your boots or dry clay that crumbles to dust. Digging in these conditions destroys the soil structure necessary to maintain air pockets and rooting channels.

▶ **Organics:** When safe to do so, break up surface with a fork to alleviate compaction and work in barrow-loads of

Top Tip
Fork sides and base of a generous planting hole to avoid it acting as a sump and filling with water.

straw-based manure. The natural chemicals released help the minute clay particles cluster together, creating a friable crumb structure and encouraging earthworm activity.

▶ **Mulching:** Mulch between plants with bulky, well-rotted organic matter.

▶ **Drainage:** Raise the profile of the border, heaping up soil to create a ridge. Plant on the higher parts.

Clay Companions

Happily, there are many attractive shrubs and perennials that thrive on clay. Establish some of these to help improve soil quality and drainage:

Perennials

▶ *Anemone x hybrida* (Japanese anemone)
▶ *Aster* (Michaelmas daisy)
▶ *Bergenia* (elephant's ears)
▶ *Geranium* (cranesbill)
▶ hosta
▶ *Leucanthemum* (Shasta daisy)
▶ *Lysimachia punctata* (yellow loosestrife)
▶ *Monarda* (bee balm)
▶ *Sedum spectabile* (ice plant)
▶ *Solidago* (goldenrod)
▶ *Persicaria* (knotweed)

Shrubs

▶ *Berberis* (barberry)
▶ *Chaenomeles* (Japanese quince)
▶ *Cornus alba* (dogwood)
▶ cotoneaster
▶ *Escallonia*
▶ *Euonymus fortunei*
▶ forsythia
▶ hydrangea
▶ *Philadelphus* (mock orange)
▶ *Physocarpus opulifolius* (ninebark)
▶ *Prunus laurocerasus* (cherry laurel)
▶ roses
▶ *Sambucus* (elder)
▶ *Spiraea*
▶ *Viburnum opulus, V. tinus* and others

129

Damp and Bog Gardens

Draining a damp garden is not the cheapest option. Permanently damp borders can support lush foliage and some beautifully sculpted blooms and the range of moisture lovers is in fact fairly substantial. Surprisingly there are trees and shrubs that survive quite happily with their roots in damp soil though take care with willows which can damage drains and building foundations. Some herbaceous perennials may need extra protection in winter if they originate from sub-tropical regions although most plants look after themselves.

Moisture Gardening

Even if you don't have a pool or wildlife pond, the luxuriant foliage and moist soil conditions found in damp borders and bog gardens create ideal habitat for amphibians and certain reptiles. Slugs and other prey abound in moist shade and in winter, the thick vegetation layer provides thermal protection for frogs, toads and newts. In spring, once leaves start to grow, cut back dead material and mulch plants with well-rotted manure.

Top Tip
Make a giant parcel by folding the umbrella-like leaves of the tender Brazilian rhubarb *Gunnera manicata* over the crown to protect from frost.

130

Shrubs for Damp Borders

The following ornamental foliage and coloured-stemmed shrubs will add height and colour to damp borders:

- *Carex alba* 'Sibirica' (Siberian dogwood)
- *Carex alba* 'Spaethii' (variegated dogwood)
- *Clethra alnifolia* (sweet pepper bush)
- *Salix alba var vitellina* 'Britzensis' (coral bark willow)

Sunny and Moist

Most of the following colourful perennials will also grow in partial shade:

Iris laevigata (Japanese Iris)

- Astilbe
- *Carex elata* 'Aurea' (Bowles' golden sedge)
- *Filipendula palmata* 'Rubra' (red meadowsweet)
- *Houttuynia cordata* 'Chameleon'
- *Iris laevigata* cultivars (Japanese iris)
- *Iris pseudocorus* 'Variegata'
- *Ligularia* 'The Rocket'
- *Lythrum salicaria* 'Feuerkerze'/ 'Firecandle' (purple loosestrife)
- *Primula bulleyana, P. x bulleesiana* (candelabra primulas)
- variegated hostas

Damp Shade

The perennials and ferns listed below enjoy wet woodland but will also grow in damp soils shaded by buildings, their sculptural qualities complementing the architecture:

- *Darmera pelata* (umbrella plant)
- *Gunnera manicata*
- Hosta
- *Matteuccia struthiopteris* (shuttlecock fern)
- *Osmunda regalis* (royal fern)
- *Rheum palmatum* 'Atrosanguineum' (ornamental rhubarb)
- *Rodgersia pinnata* and *R. aesculifolia*
- *Zantedeschia aethiopica* 'Crowborough'

131

Sandy Soils

In contrast to 'heavy' soils like clay, light, sandy soils cannot hold on to water. Not only does this create drought issues, it also makes the ground poor in nutrients. This is a particular problem after a wet winter, when minerals like calcium are washed out of the topsoil and sandy ground can become more acidic. Sands often occur by the coast and may have been deposited elsewhere during glaciation or develop above sandstone bedrock. The natural vegetation tends to be dry grassland with acid-loving shrubs such as heather and gorse.

Acid-requiring rhododendrons and heather grow well on mulched sandy soils

Working with Sand

A well cared for sandy soil warms up quickly in spring so that you can get ahead with tasks like sowing hardy annual flowers and vegetables. It is generally easy to cultivate though sometimes hard layers occur which need to be broken up. But after planting, the best policy is to leave it alone and simply add more organic matter as deep mulches every year in late winter.

Top Tip

Acid soils restrict the range of plants you can grow. Do a pH test in spring to see how acidic the soil is after winter. Adding lime (not at the same time as organic mulch), or sustainably sourced calcified seaweed, brings the pH level up but you need to do this in stages guided by frequent pH testing.

Mulching and Feeding

Mulching with well-rotted animal manure has the following advantages:

▶ Stabilizes surface and stops fine grains blowing away.
▶ Creates a deep, moist rooting layer, especially important on thin soils.
▶ Keeps nutrients near the surface preventing loss when it rains.
▶ Seals in moisture.

You can feed sandy soils exclusively with good quality organic mulches or other products including:

▶ Home-made compost.
▶ Animal manure.
▶ Spent mushroom compost (contains lime).
▶ Pelleted chicken manure or fish, blood and bone (spring topdressing).
▶ Seaweed (if you have legal access this can be dug in fresh as a natural fertilizer).

Plants for Sand

For dry sunny borders use plants recommended in Seaside Gardens (*see* page 140). For shady acidic borders choose relevant plants from Woodland Effects and Acid Soils (see pages 126–27, 134–135).

The drought-tolerant *Cytisus* (broom) tolerates poor sand

133

Acid Soils

Many gardeners hanker after acid soil and the chance to grow some of the finest shrubs and trees, including rhododendrons and azaleas and properly blue hydrangeas. Even before you carry out a pH test on your soil, having a wander about the neighbourhood and seeing if you can spot healthy specimens of these and other plants listed below, should give you an idea. Some acid soils such as heath and moorland or thin sandy types, can be quite poor. Acid clays are richer though possibly poorly drained.

Growing and Using Acid Lovers

Light dappled shade suits many acid lovers as they typically originate in wooded areas where the soil is made up of broken down leaf litter or conifer needles. This moisture-retaining, yet free-draining mix is the ideal soil to emulate when growing shade-loving members of the erica family (*Ericaceae*) and other woodlanders. The sun-loving heathers come from heaths and moors where sphagnum moss bogs have created peat.

Overcoming Cultivation Problems

Apply deep mulches every year of organic matter that does not

Did You Know?

It isn't the iron in soils but the amount of aluminium a plant is able to absorb that turns hydrangeas blue. On alkaline soils, hydrangeas can't absorb the aluminium salt so blooms remain pink or red. Even on acid soils, it can take hydrangeas several years to go true blue. Speed the process with Hydrangea Colourant which is available from garden centres.

134

contain lime (spent mushroom compost does). This maintains the moisture-holding capacity of soils, especially free-draining acid sands. In borderline pH conditions, some plants may show signs of nutrient deficiency or chlorosis, where the veins are dark green and the rest of the leaf is yellow. Treat with seaweed tonic and sequestered iron.

Ericaceous and Other Acid Lovers

The following plants must have acid soil (ericaceous) and are marked with an asterisk. Others prefer neutral to acid conditions. Perennials and annuals are less fussy about pH than shrubs.

Skimmia

Shrubs

- *Acer palmatum* (Japanese maple)
- *Camellia**
- *Erica* (most) and *Calluna vulgaris* (heathers)*
- *Gaultheria procumbens* and *G. mucronata* cultivars*
- *Hydrangea*
- *Kalmia latifolia**
- *Leucothoe**
- *Pieris**
- *Rhododendron* (rhododendron and azalea)*
- *Skimmia*

Perennials and Alpines

- *Gentiana sino-ornata* (gentian)*
- *Lithodora diffusa* 'Heavenly Blue' (syn Lithospermum)*
- *Meconopsis betonicifolia* (Tibetan blue poppy)*

Meconopsis betonicifolia

Chalky Soils

Ground overlying chalk or limestone can appear pale with chunks of white rock or flint nodules often visible on the surface. These soils are markedly alkaline or in gardening parlance 'sweet' as opposed to 'sour' (acidic soils). Depending on the geological history of an area, some gardeners will find themselves with thin, stony and free-draining soil while others could have poorly drained clay deposited on the bedrock. Many chalk and limestone plants are sun-lovers, and chalk enables rich wildflower communities to develop which in turn support healthy bee and butterfly populations.

Careful Planting

A much greater range of plants will grow on alkaline or chalky soils than on acid ones and with some improvement to alkaline clay, you could create a conventional mixed border of colourful, easily obtained shrubs, perennials, bulbs and annuals. But on thin, sharply drained ground, you might want to take the opportunity to create a special feature using drought-tolerant lime lovers, such as a rock garden or

Mediterranean-style gravel-mulched border. With a larger space you could also accommodate an annual mini wildflower meadow.

Improving Conditions

Certain plants develop iron or magnesium deficiency in limy soils, the telltale signs being an unhealthy pallor and dark green veins with yellow in between (*see* Acid Soils page 134, for treatment). Work in copious amounts of well-rotted manure into the top fork depth of chalky clay and also mulch after planting (*see* Clay Soils page 128).

Lavandula (lavender)

Plants for Mixed Borders

▶ *Achillea millefolium* (yarrow)

▶ *Anchusa azurea* 'Loddon Royalist'

▶ *Campanula glomerata* 'Superba'

▶ *Ceanothus* (Californian lilac)

▶ *Centranthus ruber* (red valerian)

▶ *Ceratostigma* (hardy plumbago)

▶ *Chaenomeles* (Japanese quince)

▶ *Dianthus* 'Mrs Sinkins'

▶ *Gypsophila paniculata* (baby's breath)

▶ *Knautia macedonica*

▶ *Verbascum* (mullein)

▶ *Verbena bonariensis* (purple-top vervain)

▶ *Scabiosa caucasica* 'Clive Greaves'

▶ *Sisyrinchium striatum*

Alpines and Mediterranean Shrubs

▶ *Allium christophii*

▶ *Campanula carpatica*

▶ *Lavandula* (lavender)

▶ *Pulsatilla vulgaris* (Pasque flower)

▶ *Rosmarinus officinalis* (rosemary)

▶ *Santolina chamaecyparissus* (cotton lavender)

▶ *Saponaria ocymoides*

▶ *Veronica umbrosa* 'Georgia Blue'

137

Poor, Thin Soils

If you are the sort of person who loves luxuriant borders planted with colourful shrubs and perennials, moving to a site with poor, thin soil can be disappointing. Mountain soils and ground in old mining and quarrying areas is typically stony and shallow, difficult to dig and you often hit solid rock just below the surface. High rainfall may also wash away what little nutrients there are. With the right varieties though and some clever planting strategies, you can create a garden to be proud of.

Allium

Improving Your Lot

An initial survey is useful to work out where the best layers of topsoil are. In some places most of it may have been removed, or eroded away naturally by the elements. Here there will be only poor vegetation cover and even weeds may struggle. In other areas there could be bare rock outcrops but with deeper pockets of good soil between. Importing tonnes of topsoil and creating terraces to accommodate larger root balls and to stop soil being washed away down a slope is effective, but also expensive.

Planting on a Slope

Prevent the rootball becoming exposed through soil erosion by making a flat area with a crescent-shaped supporting 'wall' of stones or shaped earth covered in pegged-down hessian or plastic mesh. Dig a generous planting hole and improve the infill by mixing in manure or garden compost. Alternatively, peg down weed matting and plant through with prostrate conifers, especially junipers and pines and other robust creeping shrubs like cotoneaster whose roots stabilize the ground.

Cotoneaster

Top Tip

Annual surface applications of 10cm (4 inch) deep, well-rotted farm or stable manure, work wonders. Mulching not only increases fertility but also improves conditions for earthworms and other vital soil organisms as well as retaining moisture.

Tough Cookies

The following plants should be used where it's difficult to improve soil conditions:

▶ Hardy alpines including *Sempervivum*.
▶ Mediterranean herbs e.g. lavender (ideal for thin soils over limestone. See above).
▶ Tussock-forming grasses and sedges (many).
▶ Hardy annuals (many).
▶ Species tulips, crocus, alliums (for gravel soils in full sun).

139

Seaside Gardens

Being near the sea is a mixed blessing. On one hand the proximity of the water means that winters tend to be far milder than inland and you can often grow tender and sub-tropical plants. The downside is that salt-laden winds can scorch plants and many common garden varieties simply can't cope with the conditions.

Planting by the Coast

There are certain common characteristics to vegetation around coastlines. Dune and seaside plants are often protected from wind and salt damage by a waxy coating that makes blades glossy or turns them blue-green. Another strategy is a grey woolly or felted covering. Smaller leaves also cuts moisture loss. Soils may be thin and sandy. *See* page 132 for improving sandy soils.

Seaside Shrubs

A deep border or shelter-belt of tough trees and shrubs protects the garden from prevailing winds and is often more effective than a man-made fence. Combine wind- and salt-resistant plants:

▶ *Brachyglottis* Dunedin Hybrids

▶ Cotoneaster

▶ *Elaeagnus x ebbingei*

▶ *Escallonia*

▶ *Hippophae rhamnoides* (sea buckthorn)

▶ *Juniperus* (junipers)

▶ *Olearia macrodonta* (daisy bush)

▶ *Pinus sylvestris* 'Watereri'

▶ *Pyracantha* (firethorn)

▶ *Rosa rugosa*

▶ *Tamarix* (tamarisk)

▶ *Viburnum tinus* (laurustinus)

Within the sheltered zone grow other salt-tolerant plants including:

▶ *Cordyline australis* (cabbage palm)

▶ *Cytisus* and *Genista* (broom)

▶ *Euonymus fortunei* and *E. japonicus*

▶ evergreen herbs

▶ *Griselinia littoralis*

▶ hardy fuchsia

▶ *Hebe*

▶ *Hydrangea macrophylla* and *H. paniculata*

▶ *Olearia x hastii*

▶ *Phormium*

▶ *Yucca*

Perennials and Annuals

Evergreen grasses, carpeting succulents, dune and clifftop plants can be used to create a naturalistic shingle garden in a sunny spot. Try planting:

▶ *Anemanthele lessoniana* (pheasant tail grass)

▶ annual poppies

▶ *Armeria maritima* (thrift)

▶ *Centranthus ruber* (red valerian)

▶ *Crambe maritima* (sea kale)

▶ *Eschscholzia* (Californian poppy)

▶ *Eryngium* (sea holly)

▶ *Euphorbia myrsinites* (spurge)

▶ *Festuca glauca* cultivars (blue fescue)

▶ *Libertia*

▶ *Sedum* (stonecrop)

▶ *Verbascum* (mullein)

Kniphofia
(red hot poker)

In conventional borders mix the above plants with hardy perennials including:

▶ *Achillea* (yarrow)

▶ *agapanthus*

▶ *Bergenia* (elephant's ears)

▶ *Crocosmia*

▶ *Geranium* (cranesbill)

▶ *Hemerocallis* (daylily)

▶ *Kniphofia* (red hot poker)

▶ *Nepeta x faassenii* (catmint)

▶ *Penstemon*

▶ *Stachys byzantina* 'Silver Carpet' (lamb's ears)

Sunny and Sheltered

Having a warm, sheltered, microclimate may mean that you can grow frost-sensitive plants outdoors all year round. Your choice of shrubs, climbers and perennials is also much wider than most gardeners could consider. Your garden could benefit from the warming effect of an urban environment, proximity to the sea or a large lake. Or walls and buildings might shelter your plot and trap the heat given out by paving and brickwork. Dry ground could be a problem in low rainfall areas but many of the plants recommended below are drought tolerant.

Exotics like *Heliconia* need overwintering indoors

Planting with Exotica

Some tender plants have a striking architectural form that makes them look subtropical and rather alien compared to common garden plants. They don't always mix well with say cottage garden perennials and larger specimens may also need more space around them to display their features properly. A contemporary arrangement of plants contrasted with rounded boulders and pebbles and a mulch of gravel can be a more satisfying approach visually when working with grasses and sculptural succulents. Flowering wall shrubs and climbers are less tricky to place. Most need good drainage and full sun.

142

Tree fern

Tender Wall Shrubs and Climbers

The following plants are best sheltered and/or supported by a wall. They may need watering in the growing season.

▶ *Abutilon x suntense* 'Jermyns'
▶ *Callistemon citrinus* 'Splendens' (bottlebrush)
▶ *Campsis x tagliabuana* 'Madame Galen'
▶ *Carpenteria californica*
▶ *Ceanothus* 'Concha' and others (Californian lilac)
▶ *Cytisus battandieri* (Moroccan broom)
▶ *Escallonia* 'Iveyi'
▶ *Fremontodendron californicum* 'California Glory' – CARE: irritant hairs
▶ *Magnolia grandiflora* 'Exmouth' and others
▶ *Passiflora caerulea* (passion flower)
▶ *Solanum crispum* and *S. laxum*
▶ *Trachelospermum jasminoides* (star jasmine)

Stand-Alone Specimens

Provided the following sculptural plants are in a sheltered spot they can be grown in a more isolated position or away from a wall.

▶ *Astelia chathamica* (silver spear)
▶ *Chamaerops humilis* (dwarf European palm)
▶ *Cordyline australis* 'Albertii' (cabbage palm)
▶ *Dicksonia* or *Cyathea* (tree fern) – needs shade
▶ *Eryobotrya japonica* (loquat)
▶ *Euphorbia mellifera* (honey spurge)
▶ *Fascicularia bicolor* (a moderately hardy bromeliad)
▶ *Lobelia tupa*
▶ *Melianthus major*
▶ *Pittosporum tobira*

Callistemon citrinus (bottlebrush)

Windy and Exposed

Most gardeners have a few challenges to contend with but making a garden in a windy location is one of the toughest. Wind strips moisture from plant foliage, shreds large leaves and also rocks plants, loosening their roots and sometimes even pushing them over. Without a filter to reduce the impact of strong winds, newly planted specimens take much longer to establish and 'soft' plants like annual bedding may just wither.

Barberries make tough shelter plants

Shelter and Planting

Solid boundaries like fences often create turbulence and in any case may not withstand strong gusts. It is far better if you have room, to plant a hedge or a deep band of mixed trees and shrubs called a shelter belt. This filters the wind and can protect a much wider area from damage. It pays to plant small young specimens as opposed to older, larger shrubs and trees as the former establish more easily and often overtake.

Getting Plants Established

There are several things you can do to help establish plants in windy borders:

▶ Surround with 50 per cent windbreak mesh fixed to wooden posts.

▶ Use transparent plastic tree and shrub shelters for saplings and hedging.

▶ Stake shrubs and use two or more stakes for trees to hold the bottom third solidly.

▶ Apply a deep organic mulch around new plantings to retain moisture and help build a strong root system.

Hedges filter and slow down strong winds

Wind-Tolerant Plantings

Many of the plants listed under Seaside Gardens (*see* pages 140–41) as well as under Dry and Sunny (*see* pages 122–23) are useful in windy but bright conditions provided the general climate isn't too cold. Planting a background structure of wind-resistant plants within a border provides shelter for more vulnerable plants that can be added when enough cover has been established. Consider planting mixed screens and border backdrops of wild black cherry (*Prunus serotina*); birch (*Betula*); hazel (*Corylus*); barberry (*Berberis*); beech (*Fagus*), holly (*Ilex aquifolium*), pine (e.g. *Pinus sylvestris*) tamarisk (*Tamarix*) and sea buckthorn (*Hippophae rhamnoides*).

Cold Gardens

In geographic regions affected by cold winters, gardeners are limited to growing bone hardy plants. Check minimum temperatures for your part of the world before selecting plants. Cold spots also occur

Alpine plants work well in cold spots

within milder areas depending on a garden's position and elevation. A plot on the north side of a hill will be colder than one facing south. Cold air sinks to the bottom of any slope and pools if it can't escape. A dense hedge might prevent cold air dissipating on a chilly night and this 'frost pocket' can kill tender specimens.

Choosing Plants

Landscape borders in cold spots with the following plant types:

▶ Hardy deciduous trees and shrubs (these are generally more resilient than evergreens).

▶ Cold-tolerant conifers.

▶ Herbaceous perennials including hardy bulbs (most can tough it out because they disappear below ground through winter).

▶ Hardy annuals and half-hardy bedding plants – useful for providing summer colour as their growth is unaffected by cold in the growing season.

▶ Most creeping and cushion-forming alpines.

Did You Know?

If you look at the trees and hedges in an exposed area they are bent away from the prevailing wind. They grow like this to create an aerodynamic profile that allows wind to blow over them without damaging them further.

Checklist

▶ **Growing conditions:** Gather info locally on climate, soil and suitable plantings.

▶ **Sunny borders:** Use Mediterranean herbs, alpines and bulbs for dry, sunny borders.

▶ **Shade:** Improve conditions for dry shade with deep mulches.

▶ **Woodland:** For a woodland effect, create tiered plantings beneath the canopy.

▶ **Clay beds:** Avoid working wet or very dry clay. Improve with bulky organic matter. Plant clay borders with plants that withstand summer drought/winter water-logging.

▶ **Damp borders:** Select lush, moisture-loving perennials and ferns for damp borders.

▶ **Sandy soils:** Improve moisture-holding capacity and fertility of sandy soils with organic mulches plus fertilizers/lime applied after winter rains.

▶ **Tailored planting:** Plant shaded sandy borders with woodland or acid-loving plants (check pH). Use seaside plants for sun.

▶ **Acidic soil:** Plant acidic soils with ericaceous or plants preferring neutral to acid pH.

▶ **Vitamin boost:** Treat plants suffering nutrient deficiency due to extreme acid/alkaline conditions with sequestered iron.

▶ **Chalky soil:** Plant lime- and drought-tolerant plants on thin chalky soils.

▶ **Seaside:** Use salt- and wind-tolerant plants in seaside borders.

▶ **Hot and cold:** Pick hardy deciduous shrubs, herbaceous, alpines and bulbs for cold gardens. Take advantage of warm, sheltered sites to grow 'exotica'.

Border

Styles

Modern Mixed Borders

For most gardeners, the combination of flowering and foliage shrubs and herbaceous and evergreen perennials produces the ideal border. Mixed plantings have only moderate maintenance requirements and repay a little tender loving care with an abundance of colour. With the right plant selections, mixed borders can have plenty of structure and interest even in the winter months, and spring- and early-summer flowering bulbs, spring bedding plants and biennials such as sweet William bridge the seasons nicely.

Building Blocks

Structure comes in the form of small ornamental trees, conifers, shrubs and trained forms. These last might be clipped shrubs or topiary figures, or climbers trained over supports. A permanent framework adds height and form that satisfies the eye even in the dormant season. Using this structure to hold the display together, you can then flow in ephemeral

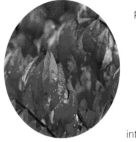

*Euonymus
alatus*

plants like herbaceous perennials, ornamental grasses, bulbs and annuals. Make your mixed borders as mannered or wild as you like; it's your choice.

Deciduous v Evergreen

It's tempting to choose only plants which hold on to their leaves in an attempt to maintain interest year round and to avoid bare patches. But in practice, mixing deciduous and evergreen plants produces a more dynamic and visually interesting display. Depending on your choice, deciduous plants have a number of attractions and benefits including:

▶ Autumn leaf tints

▶ Colourful winter stems

▶ Bright new leaves or emerging shoots

▶ Seasonal transformations e.g. from bud to flower to seed head or fruit, or, changing foliage colour through the year

▶ Hardiness

Seasonal Highlights

To get the most out of a mixed border there should be numerous seasonal peaks. These could take the form of a swathe of bright yellow spring daffodils and purple heathers or a single spectacular shrub like *Ceanothus* 'Puget Blue' bursting into bloom against a wall in early summer. High-season roses and flowering perennials make another

151

wave and berrying or smouldering foliage plants are quite capable of stealing the show in autumn.

Colour Components

Whether your preference is for a muted palette or strong, eye-catching shades, you'll need plants that provide colour either through leaves, flowers, stems or fruits. Go for long-lasting elements, especially in small gardens where plants have to work twice as hard to earn their space. Don't forget vertical features such as a blossom tree or flowering climber and carpet the ground with a tapestry of perennials, herbs and low shrubs.

Showy Shrubs and Climbers

Some long-flowering shrubs and colourful foliage plants fit perfectly with herbaceous perennials and annuals in a mixed border setting. Remember to choose plants according to your specific soil type and aspect. For example rhododendrons and azaleas, camellias, pieris and Leucothoe all need acid soil and often prefer dappled shade. The following provide months of flower or foliage interest:

- ▶ *Berberis thunbergii* 'Rose Glow'
- ▶ *Ceanothus x delineanus* 'Gloire de Versailles'
- ▶ *Clematis* 'Madame Julia Correvon'
- ▶ *Cornus alba* 'Gouchaultii'
- ▶ *Hydrangea arborescens* 'Annabelle'
- ▶ *Hydrangea paniculata* 'Pink Diamond

▶ *Lavatera x clementii* 'Rosea' (shrubby mallow)

▶ *Mahonia x media* 'Winter Sun'

Modern Roses

Rose breeding has come a long way in recent years and so has the way we grow roses. Compact, disease resistant bush roses (floribundas and hybrid teas) as well as modern climbers are ideal for the mixed border. Few flowering shrubs bloom over such a long period or have fragrant flowers (some) and endless shades to choose from. There are also miniature and patio roses (petite repeat-flowering bush roses) to suit really small spaces.

Long-lasting Perennials

If you want a more carefree look for your mixed borders, concentrate on herbaceous and evergreen perennials that don't need staking or regular lifting and dividing and that flower or have beautiful foliage displays for months. Consider the following collection of easy-care plants:

▶ *Anemone x hybrida* 'Honorine Jobert'

▶ *Artemisia ludoviciana* 'Valerie Finnis' (mugwort)

▶ *Aster x frikartii* 'Mönch' (Michaelmas daisy)

▶ *Chelone obliqua* (turtle head)

▶ *Geranium* (cranesbill) e.g. 'Dragon Heart'

▶ *Hemorocallis* (day lily) e.g. 'Stella de Oro'

▶ *Heuchera* 'Licorice'

▶ *Iris sibirica*

▶ *Leucanthemum* 'Goldrush' or 'Goldrausch' (yellow Shasta daisy)

▶ *Penstemon* 'Andenken an Friedrich Hahn'

▶ *Salvia x sylvestris* 'Mainacht'

Penstemon

153

Herbaceous Borders

Many of the surviving Victorian and Edwardian estate gardens have traditional herbaceous borders that once took large teams of gardeners to manage. Typically these are long, deep beds backed by a very high wall or clipped hedge. Strongly associated with herbaceous borders, the Edwardian garden designer Gertrude Jekyll still wields influence today. She left her mark not only in the impressionistic way that she 'painted' with herbaceous perennials but also in her application of the artist's colour wheel when combining plants.

Power Behind the Flower

In full swing, traditional herbaceous borders are an impressive sight, and there's no reason why you couldn't manage a cut-down version in your own plot. Flowers are seductive and the vision of a border full of perennials is tempting. But before you embark on a project, estimate how much time and effort you have to devote to it. Many classic varieties flower so profusely that they need regular lifting and dividing to keep them healthy and vigorous. Use labour-saving techniques to ease the workload and pick modern, trouble-free varieties.

High Maintenance Alternatives

Traditional herbaceous plantings included many tall and medium-sized perennials that mostly needed staking. The requirement for height was due to the scale of the deep borders with their tall backdrops. Penstemons, day lilies and cranesbills rarely need staking and the following tall but self-supporting perennials add drama. Try the following:

- ▶ *Acanthus spinosus* (bear's breeches)
- ▶ *Alcea rosea* 'Nigra' (black hollyhock)
- ▶ *Cynara cardunculus* (cardoon)
- ▶ *Echinops ritro* (globe thistle)
- ▶ *Macleaya cordata* (plume poppy)
- ▶ *Sidalcea* 'William Smith'
- ▶ *Verbascum* 'Gainsborough' (mullein)
- ▶ *Veronicastrum virginicum*

Iris 'Jane Phillips'

Echinops ritro (globe thistle)

Herbaceous plants may need copious watering in dry spells so apply deep organic mulches that also provide 'fuel' for their rapid development.

Low Water Bed

Fortunately there are plants like the reliable tall bearded iris 'Jane Phillips', ornamental onions (*Allium*) and perennial wallflower (*Erysimum* 'Bowles's Mauve') that perform even in hot, dry summers or on very free-draining soils. They can also be used in mixed borders to cut down on watering. *See* pages 122–25 for more examples.

155

New Perennial Planting

In recent years there has been a move to more naturalistic styles of planting using largely perennials. Sometimes called prairie-style gardening, advocates of the new perennial landscape movement typically combine well-behaved ornamental grasses with drought-tolerant, easy-care herbaceous perennials and sub-shrubs (plants with a woody base but soft shoots). The technique is perfect for owners of larger gardens wanting to cut down on workload, as maintenance is minimal.

A Bit of History

William Robinson, Edwardian author of *The Wild Garden*, was considered maverick for advocating the use of hardy perennials and natives in a way that mirrored natural vegetation. Today his ideas have been developed further by the internationally renowned Dutch plant designer Piet Oudalf as well as the Washington-based landscape architects Oehme and van Sweden.

How to Do It

The main idea is to enjoy the seasonal progression of perennials from the time they emerge through to flowering and seed production before they die down. Plants that have a good winter presence, either in the form of mummified flowers and seed heads, or dry stems and foliage, are essential. In spring, once deciduous grasses have started to re-grow at the base, simply cut the whole lot down and apply general fertilizer.

- ▶ Use a matrix of tall ornamental grasses or sedges on their own or combined with a restricted palette of flowering perennials.

- ▶ In places you can try planting large swathes of one plant.

156

▶ Pick drought- and cold-resistant forms.

▶ Include 'prairie' perennials and near relatives of wild plants.

Rudbeckia fulgida (black-eyed Susan)

Grasses and Sedges

The following plants are ideal for prairie-style or new perennial planting, having a long season of interest and the required soft, 'see-through' quality.

▶ *Calamagrostis x acutiflora* 'Karl Foerster'
▶ *Carex flagellifera*
▶ *Deschampsia caespitosa*
▶ *Miscanthus sinensis*
▶ *Molinea caerulea* subsp. *arundinacea*
▶ *Panicum virgatum*
▶ *Stipa calamagrostis, S. gigantea, S. tenuissima*

Prairie-style Flowers

Plant a combination of classic daisy-flowered prairie species like black-eyed Susan (*Rudbeckia fulgida*), purple cone flower (*Echinacea purpurea*) and taller tickseeds (*Coreopsis species*), as well as Kansas gayfeather (*Liatris spicata*) and Joe Pye weed (*Eupatorium maculatum* Atropurpureum Group). Other plants to try include:

▶ *Achillea millefolium* cultivars (yarrow)
▶ *Perovskia atriplicifolia* 'Blue Spire'
▶ *Sedum* 'Herbstfreude'
▶ *Verbena bonariensis*

Calamagrostis x acutiflora (feather reed grass)

157

Easy-care Shrub Borders

Borders with hardy shrubs and ground cover plants are easy to maintain and with bark mulching might only need a couple of days' work a year. Depending on where you live and the local microclimate, you could have a foliage display that feels distinctly sub-tropical with hardy palms such as Cordyline, New Zealand flax (*Phormium*) or Fatsia japonica. Alternatively in shady acid soil, the bed could have a refined woodland look. Shrub borders may peak during winter or spring, but you can also create colourful, year-round displays too.

Create a sub-tropical feel with hardy architectural evergreens

Layered Planting

In a small, narrow bed you might use dwarf and creeping shrubs but in larger areas, tiered arrangements of small trees and larger shrubs working down to low growing specimens and ground cover, creates more interest. Use smaller shrubs in clusters of the same variety for greater impact, and bring a few tall, narrow plants like the pencil slim conifer *Juniperus scopulorum* 'Blue Arrow' forward to break up the lines.

Top Flowering Shrubs

Modern, disease-resistant shrub roses make excellent additions to any garden.

Try *Rosa rugosa* forms and repeat-flowering English roses. The ground-cover rose 'Flower Carpet' provides long-lasting colour. Other strong types are *Choisya x dewitteana* 'Aztec Pearl', winter-flowering skimmia, hardy fuchsias and repeat-flowering pink-deepening-to-burgundy Hydrangea 'Preziosa', with purple-tinged foliage.

Leaf Colour

The following shrubs provide year-round interest through their foliage. Ones marked with an asterisk require acid soil. Remember to vary texture, leaf shape and overall habit of adjacent plants just as you would in a mixed border.

Photinia

Tall

- *Elaeagnus x Ebbingei* 'Limelight'
- *Photinia x fraseri* 'Red Robin'
- *Pieris* 'Forest Flame' *
- *Physocarpus opulifolius* 'Dart's Gold'
- *Sambucus nigra* 'Eva' ('Black Lace')

Medium

- *Abelia x grandiflora* 'Frances Mason'
- *Choisya ternata* 'Sundance'
- *Fuchsia magellanica* 'Versicolor'
- *Leucothoe fontanesiana* 'Rainbow' *
- *Nandina domestica*

Small

- *Berberis thunbergii* 'Bagatelle'
- *Euonymus fortunei* 'Emerald 'n' Gold'
- *Lavandula angustifolia* 'Hidcote'
- *Leucothoe* 'Scarletta' *
- *Weigela* 'Naomi Campbell'

Top Tip

Use bright, evergreen ground cover e.g. *Vinca minor* 'Illumination' for weed-suppression, under-planted with dwarf daffodils for an extra lift in the spring.

159

Cottage Garden Borders

Originally cottage gardens contained all the food, medicinal and dye plants necessary for survival, while the flowers attracted bees for fruit and vegetable pollination or aided honey production. Fragrant plants masked the smell of farm animals occupying the same small plot. A modern interpretation of a cottage garden can reflect these roots in the layout and choice of plants. Writer Margery Fish revived the cottage garden during the second half of the twentieth century with her famous garden at East Lambrook Manor in Somerset.

A Heady Mix

A hugely appealing aspect of cottage gardening today is the chaotic mix of edible plants, herbs and ornamentals and the way that so much can be crammed into a small plot. If you don't have room for a separate productive area or herb garden, this is an ideal approach. Cottage plants and the way in which they are intermingled, also favour wildlife and beneficial insects, helping to keep pest problems to a minimum.

Pretty Fruit and Vegetables

If you are going to mix edibles with your flowers, it makes sense to choose plants that look and taste good. Include:

Runner beans

- ▶ **Fruit trees:** Try pears and plums on dwarfing rootstocks and step-over apples.

- ▶ **Soft fruit bushes:** Plant gooseberry, redcurrant and on acid soil, blueberry.

- ▶ **Strawberries:** Use as border edging (wild, 'fraises des bois' types as well as cultivated).

- ▶ **Beans:** Wigwams of runner beans with coloured flowers e.g. 'Painted Lady'.

- ▶ **Climbers:** Try edible yet ornamental climbers like golden hop (*Humulus lupulus* 'Aureus'), grape vine, squash and thornless blackberry.

- ▶ **Salad:** Choose coloured leaf lettuce, ruby chard and beetroot 'Bull's Blood'.

- ▶ **Vegetables:** Try purple-podded dwarf French bean 'Purple Teepee' and yellow courgettes.

Top Tip

Many garden flowers are poisonous e.g. aconite, delphinium, foxglove and numerous bulb blooms.

Edible Flowers

Grow your own garnishes, cake decorations and salad ingredients. Pick flowers and petals from viola, day lily (*Hemerocallis*), pot marigold (*Calendula officinalis*), rose, sunflower (*Helianthus annuus*), lavender, scented pelargoniums, nasturtium (*Tropaeolum majus*) and most herbs e.g. chives, borage, fennel, mint and marjoram.

161

Convallaria majalis
(lily-of-the-valley)

Wild Relatives

Everything from the woodbine (honeysuckle) round the door to the sweet violets and hose-in-hose primulas under the apple tree would have originally been selected from local woodland, hedgerow and meadow plants. Some of the best-loved cottage blooms are only a few steps away from their wild ancestors. One reason why some old varieties persist today is that they are hardy, disease resistant and easy to grow.

Cottage Scents

Along with fragrant shrubs such as lavender, winter- and spring-flowering viburnums, lilac and mock orange (*Philadelphus*) and climbers like rambler roses and jasmine, are a host of sweetly scented annual, biennial, perennial and bulb blooms, still retaining their original 'wild' fragrance. Among the best are:

▶ *Convallaria majalis* (lily-of-the-valley)

▶ *Dianthus* (clove-scented pinks)

▶ *Dianthus barbatus* (sweet William)

▶ *Hesperis matronalis* (Dame's violet)

▶ *Lathyrus odoratus* (sweet pea

▶ *Lobularia maritima* (sweet alyssum)

▶ *Narcissus poeticus var. recurvus* (pheasant's eye daffodil)

▶ *Reseda odorata* (mignonette)

Iconic Blooms

Certain flowers say cottage garden like no others. Scatter some of these through your plantings to strengthen the overall look and attract bees into the bargain:

Did You Know?

Plants used for dyeing wools and fabrics often have the species name 'tinctoria' e.g. *Coreopsis, Anchusa, Anthemis* and *Genista tinctoria* (dyer's broom), and blue indigo (*Indigofera tinctoria*). Woad's latin name is *Isatis tinctoria*.

▶ *Alcea rosea* (hollyhock)

▶ *Aquilegia* (granny's bonnets)

▶ *Campanula*, including the biennial Canterbury Bells, *C. media* (bellflower)

▶ Cornfield annuals (poppy, cornflower etc.)

▶ Delphinium

▶ *Digitalis purpurea* (foxglove)

▶ *Geranium* 'Johnson's Blue' (cranesbill)

▶ *Geum* 'Mrs J Bradshaw'

▶ *Lavandula angustifolia* (English lavender)

▶ *Leucanthemum vulgare* (Ox-eye daisy) and other wild blooms e.g. *Linaria* (toadflax)

▶ *Lunaria annua* (honesty)

▶ *Malva moschata* (musk mallow)

▶ Old-fashioned or English roses

Lunaria annua
(honesty)

Hedges and Topiary

You could surround your garden with a picket fence, but a traditional hedge of woodland and hedgerow plants like hawthorn, holly or yew, clipped with a rounded top and less regard to straight lines than normal, is ideal. Work in a few topiary finials too: perhaps a stylized bird or wobbly cake-stand.

Decorative Herbs

There are numerous golden, purple or variegated forms of common herbs. Combine with good-flowering forms e.g. pink hyssop (*Hyssopus officinalis* 'Roseus'), lavenders and thymes, to enhance the cottage look. Also work in tall culinary and medicinal herbs e.g. bronze fennel, evening primrose and the daisy-flowered elecampane (*Inula helenium*).

Golden
sage

Pretty Productive

When space is at a premium and your fruit and vegetable plot is on full view, you need to make the area as attractive as possible. The layout of beds, the pattern of pathways and how the plot is contained, all matter aesthetically. Productive spaces must be practical however and, ideally, paths should be wide enough to fit a wheelbarrow and plants within easy reach for cultivation and harvest. Position water butts, greenhouses, cold frames and compost heaps close by.

Design and Planting

One approach is to make a little potager – a formal layout of raised or edged beds that creates a pleasing pattern of compartments. This could either contain salads, edible flowers, fruits and vegetables or a herb collection. You could adopt the cottage garden style (*see* pages 160–63) or simply make maximum use of trained fruits, decorative vegetable varieties and flowers for cutting, and design your productive garden as you would an ornamental plot.

Vertical Structures

Fences and walls, or posts with training wires, can be used to grow all kinds of permanent fruit trees and vines, creating a decorative divide or backdrop. Fix archways over paths to support climbing vegetables or flowers for cutting and grow the same up wooden or wicker obelisks. Try the following:

164

▶ Fan-trained cherries, peaches and figs

▶ Espalier apples and pears

▶ Cordon redcurrants, cherries and apples

▶ Wire- or wall-trained blackberries, raspberries, hybrid berries and grape vines

▶ Arches and arbour seats covered with squash, climbing and runner beans, sweet peas, edible nasturtiums or vines

Border Edging

Emphasize formality and a pretty layout using low clipped box hedging alongside brick paths. In low raised beds edged with painted wooden gravel boards, plant mini hedges of dwarf lavender or clipped cotton lavender (*Santolina chamaecyparissus*) or use herbs like moss-leaved parsley, an edible flower edging of viola or pot marigold (*Calendula*) or even wild strawberry.

A Cutting Garden

Turn a sunny bed or border into an area for growing flowers for the house. Edge the bed with clipped box or, for a softer effect, lady's mantle (*Alchemilla mollis*). Grow in blocks or staked rows for ease of cutting. Include your favourites from tender perennial bulbs and tubers; tall-stemmed hardy annuals and perennials; herbs and bush roses.

165

Borders for Wildlife

With planning, even a tiny garden can become a haven for creatures from insects and other mini-beasts to amphibians, small mammals and birds. The plants you choose and the way you put them together has a big influence on how attractive the garden will be. Build on the habitats and features already in place such as tree and shrub groupings, long grass, ponds, hedges and ivy-covered walls, by adding extra attractions. You could sow nectar plants for bees, for example, and plant berrying shrubs for birds.

Increasing Food

All birds and animals need food and shelter. Small changes to the way you garden can have a positive effect on wildlife and you don't need to spend money on bird or bee houses to draw in these flying visitors. Increase the range of useful flowering and fruiting varieties and try to have some insect food-plants at the very beginning and end of the season.

Easy Upgrades

There is plenty you can do to make your garden more wildlife friendly. Here are a few ideas:

▶ **Link gardens:** Create gaps for creatures to pass through or under fences. This expands territory and food reserves.

▶ **Cover up:** Cover walls and fences with climbers and wall shrubs, especially ivy.

▶ **Wild corners:** Leave areas to long grass, weeds and wild flowers.

▶ **New shoots:** Plant a tree.

▶ **Stay green:** Make an eco-pile of prunings at the back of a border.

▶ **Winter cover:** Leave borders to die down naturally in autumn.

Woodland Style

Borders running below trees and mature shrubs could be planted to mirror woodland understory using shade-tolerant ground cover plants, leaf mulch and chipped bark to provide habitat for ground beetles and places for birds to forage. Naturalize spring-flowering bulbs, add woodland perennials and biennials like foxgloves, as well as berrying shrubs. *See* pages 126–27 for more ideas.

Waterside and Bog

Water creates an oasis effect, drawing in insects and hunting dragonflies; toads, frogs and newts seeking damp shelter and a ready food source, as well as birds who come to drink and bathe. Leaving an area of long grass and damp meadow blooms by the water, or planting an adjacent bog garden, dramatically increases the habitat value.

167

Eschscholzia californica (Californian poppy)

Meadow Appeal

Few of us have space to create a wild flower meadow but you could give a border a meadow-style makeover that would be an instant draw for insects like bees and butterflies. Perennial flower meadows work best on quite poor soils, the lack of nutrients helping to control vigorous grasses. It takes two or three years for perennial wild flower seed mixtures to bloom but while you and the bees wait, you could enjoy a show of hardy annuals. Alternatively, sow these and hardy biennials, annually for a colourful wild meadow effect.

Wild Flower Lookalikes

The following hardy annuals and bulbs will make a convincing substitute for perennial wild flowers. Choose single varieties rather than doubles to attract the most insects and sow direct or plant in sun on free-draining soil.

Annuals

▶ *Borago officinalis* (borage)

▶ *Calendula officinalis* (pot marigold)

▶ *Chrysanthemum carinatum*

▶ *Echium vulgare* 'Blue Bedder' (annual viper's bugloss)

▶ *Eschscholzia californica* (Californian poppy)

▶ *Helianthus annuus* (sunflower)

▶ *Lavatera trimestris* 'Mont Blanc'

▶ *Linum grandiflorum* 'Rubrum' (scarlet flax)

Chrysanthemum carinatum

168

- ▶ *Malope trifida* (mallowwort)
- ▶ *Nigella damascena* (love in a mist)
- ▶ *Papaver commutatum* 'Ladybird' (Caucasian scarlet poppy)
- ▶ *Papaver somniferum* (opium poppy)
- ▶ *Phacelia campanularia*

Bulbs

- ▶ *Allium hollandicum* (ornamental onion)
- ▶ *Allium sphaerocephalon* (round-headed leek)
- ▶ *Nectaroscordum siculum*
- ▶ Triumph and Darwin hybrids (tulip)

Cornfield Blooms

These plants were once common weeds of wheat fields
but seed purification and the use of herbicides virtually
eradicated them from the landscape. Cornfield annuals do
best on fertile soils and unlike most other hardy annuals, can
only germinate in the second and subsequent years if the ground is
turned over or cultivated. This makes them ideal fillers for mixed or herbaceous borders.
Try sowing the following in autumn or spring:

Did You Know?

Cornflower has been found to
stimulate the growth of wheat.
Not such a weed after all!

- ▶ *Agrostemma githago* (corn cockle)
- ▶ *Anthemis arvensis* (corn chamomile)
- ▶ *Centaurea cyanus* and the maroon black
  C. c. 'Black Ball' (cornflower)
- ▶ *Chrysanthemum segatum* (corn marigold)
- ▶ *Papaver rhoeas* (field poppy)

169

Biennial Boost

Add biennial wild flowers to a 'meadow' of hardy annuals, or supplement prairie-style plantings. The following flower in the second year from sowing:

- *Daucus carota* (wild carrot)
- *Dipsacus fullonum* (teasel)
- *Echium vulgare* (viper's bugloss)
- *Oenothera biennis* (evening primrose)
- *Salvia sclarea* (clary sage)

Did You Know?
Bumblebees shelter in foxglove flowers when it rains!

Bee Banquet

Bees are under threat the world over from urbanization and the use of agricultural and garden chemicals. And yet we cannot survive without their pollinating activities. Do your bit for bumblebees or honeybees including cultivating mixed native hedgerows as garden boundaries and being less 'tidy' in the garden. A grassy hedge base, tree root or eco-pile for example could give a queen bumblebee somewhere to hibernate over winter. A constant food supply is essential during the bee's active period which can be from late winter until the following autumn.

Seasonal Food Plants

The following plants offer a range of nectar and pollen through the growing season. Add as many as you can to your borders. Both pollen and nectar are collected. Unlike honeybees, bumblebees do not overwinter with a handy honey store so must build up their reserves in late summer and autumn and are vulnerable to starvation when they emerge in spring.

Spring

- *Aubrieta*
- *Bergenia* (elephant's ears)
- *Corylus avellana* (hazel catkins)
- Cotoneaster
- *Crocus*
- *Erica carnea, E. x darleyensis* (heather)
- Fruit tree and bush blossom
- *Galanthus* (snowdrop)
- *Hyacinthoides non-scripta* (bluebell)
- *Muscari* (grape hyacinth)
- *Myosotis* (forget-me-not)
- *Primula vulgaris* (primrose)
- *Pulmonaria*
- *Rosmarinus officinalis* (rosemary)
- *Salix* (pussy willow catkins)
- *Symphytum* (comfrey)
- *Viola* (viola and pansy)

Summer

- *Aconitum* (monkshood) – POISONOUS
- *Ajuga reptans* (bugle)
- *Alcea rosea* (hollyhock)
- *Allium* (ornamental)
- *Allium schoenoprasum* (chives)
- *Antirrhinum* (snapdragon)
- *Aquilegia* (granny's bonnets)

- *Borago officinalis* (borage)
- *Campanula* (bellflower)
- Ceanothus
- Delphinium
- *Echium vulgare* (viper's bugloss)
- *Erysimum* (perennial wallflower)
- foxglove (*Digitalis purpurea*)
- Geranium (cranesbill)
- Geum
- *Helianthus annuus* (sunflower)
- *Lavandula* (lavender)
- *Linaria purpurea* (purple loosetrife)
- *Lonicera periclymenum* (honeysuckle)
- *Lupinus* (lupin)
- *Nepeta faassenii* (catmint)
- *Papaver* (poppy)
- *Phacelia* (fiddleneck)
- *Polemonium caeruleum* (Jacob's ladder)
- *Salvia* (ornamental sage)

Late Summer-Autumn

- *Agastache foeniculum* (Anise hyssop)
- *Eupatorium* (Joe Pye weed)
- *Hedera* (ivy)
- *Rosa* (rose)
- *Scabiosa* (scabious)
- *Sedum spectabile* and 'Herbstfreude'

Lonicera periclymenum (honeysuckle)

171

Ideal Blooms

Many favourites are blue or purple. Look for the nectar spots e.g. on the throat of foxglove blooms, and streaks (nectar guides) marking a clear route to the food. Choose simple, single forms over fancy varieties which do not provide as much reward. Wild flowers and herbs are especially attractive. Bumblebees favour bell-shaped, wide-tubular or dish-shaped blooms they can easily fit into.

Butterfly Indulgence

To attract these exquisite creatures into your garden takes a little guile. Although bees will happily visit classic butterfly flowers, butterflies themselves are quite choosy. Butterflies and the much larger related group, moths, use sight (like bees they can see the ultra-violet nectar 'targets' painted on blooms), scent and taste to detect their next meal. They prefer a spacious landing platform to perch on while they probe flowers for nectar whether a fluffy spike-like Kansas gayfeather (*Liatris*) or 'thimble' of a sea holly (*Eryngium*).

Butterfly Favourites

Butterflies prefer flowers made up of many individual blooms like the centres of daisies. They also like simple flowers and thistle-like, spherical and domed-headed plants. No butterfly border would be complete without the North American perennial milkweeds (*Asclepias*) or butterfly bush (*Buddleja davidii*), hebe, lavender and Escallonia.

Top Tip

Caterpillars usually feed on the leaves of specific wild species whilst butterflies can sip from a range of nectar providers. Unless you have space for growing certain wild flowers in abundance, e.g. large swathes of nettles, it's best to cater mainly for adults.

172

Buddleja davidii (butterfly bush)

Butterfly Plants

▶ *Allium* (ornamental onions and chives)

▶ *Aster* (Michaelmas daisy)

▶ *Aubrieta*

▶ *Cardamine pratensis* (lady's smock)

▶ *Centranthus ruber* (red valerian)

▶ *Circium* (species)

▶ *Coreopsis* (tickseed)

▶ *Dianthus barbatus* (sweet William)

▶ *Echinacea* (purple cone flower)

▶ *Echinops ritro* (globe thistle)

▶ *Erysimum* (wallflower)

▶ *Eupatorium* (Joe Pye weed)

▶ *Heliotrope* (cherry pie)

▶ *Hesperis matronalis* (dame's violet)

▶ *Iberis* (candytuft)

▶ *Lantana*

▶ *Leucanthemum* (Shasta daisy)

▶ *Lunaria annua* (honesty)

▶ *Monarda* (bee balm)

▶ *Oreganum vulgare* (marjoram)

▶ *Phlox*

▶ *Rudbeckia* (black-eyed Susan)

▶ *Scabiosa* and *Knautia* (scabious)

▶ *Sedum spectabile* (ice plant)

▶ *Tagetes patula* (single French marigold)

▶ Trailing and bedding verbena

▶ *Verbena bonariensis* (purpletop vervain)

▶ *Viola* (viola and pansy)

▶ *Zinnia*

Zinnia

173

Brief Existence

Butterflies usually only live for a few months, some just a few days. A few overwinter as adults and need to fill up on late nectar to hibernate successfully, and alongside the freshly emerged spring butterflies, need a ready supply of early blooms to sustain them.

Bird Feast

Gardens with shrub and mixed borders often contain a range of natural bird food from flower buds, fruits and berries to seed heads. On a less obvious level, plants that attract insects to their flowers or are a magnet for sap-sucking pests like aphids, will also bring insect-eating species into the garden. Growing hardy berrying and fruiting shrubs not only satisfies the local population: winter migrants will frequently make a pit-stop to refuel in suburban gardens before continuing their journey. New perennial, prairie-style or meadow plantings keep seed-eating finches satisfied too.

Did You Know?
Butterflies taste through their feet.

Berrying Shrubs

You do not have to stick to native species, many birds relish the opportunity to fatten up on ornamental fruiting shrubs and trees before winter, even if berries don't normally form the bulk of their diet. Whether fruits are eaten early or late depends

Bullfinch

on location, the onset of winter and fruit and berry colour. All are eventually scoffed if it gets cold enough, but black and red tend to go first followed by orange, yellow, pink and white fruits. Try to include as many below as you have room for:

Trees

▶ *Amelanchier* (snowy mespilus)

▶ Cotoneaster

▶ *Crataegus* (hawthorn)

▶ *Ilex* (female forms) (holly)

▶ *Malus* (crab apple) e.g. 'Gorgeous'

▶ *Prunus avium* (bird cherry)

▶ *Sorbus* (rowan)

Shrubs

▶ *Berberis thunbergii* forms (barberry)

▶ *Callicarpa bodinieri var giraldii* 'Profusion' (beautyberry)

▶ *Cornus* (dogwood)

▶ Cotoneaster (shrubby and prostrate forms)

▶ *Mahonia aquifolium* (Oregon grape)

▶ *Mahonia x media* cultivars

▶ *Pyracantha* (firethorn)

▶ *Sambucus* (elder)

▶ *Viburnum opulus* (guelder rose)

▶ *Viburnum tinus* (laurustinus)

Sorbus
(rowan)

Parthenocissus tricuspidata (Boston ivy)

Climbers

▶ *Celastrus orbiculatus* Hermaphrodite Group (oriental bittersweet)

▶ *Hedera helix* (English ivy) (adult)

▶ *Lonicera periclymenum* and forms (honeysuckle)

▶ *Parthenocissus quinquefolia* (virginia creeper)

▶ *Vitis vinifera* 'Purpurea' (purple leaf grapevine)

Flower Borders

The more free and easy your garden style, the better for birds. To create food let the last crop of late summer blooms form seed heads. Though you might sacrifice some autumn colour, you will be rewarded with the sight of flocks of finches working over the plants well into winter. Try:

Perennials

▶ *Coreopsis* (tickseed)

▶ *Echinacea* (purple cone flower)

▶ *Monarda* (bee balm)

▶ *Rudbeckia* (black-eyed Susan)

▶ *Solidago* (goldenrod)

Annuals and Biennials

▶ *Amaranthus*

▶ *Centaurea cyanus* (cornflower)

▶ *Dipsacus fullonum* (teasel)

▶ *Helanthus annuus* (sunflower)

A finch dines on cone-flower seeds

Helanthus annuus
(sunflower)

Bird Habitat Planting

Birds need cover in which to escape from aerial predators as well as shelter from bad weather and a garden without trees, large shrubs or hedges is unlikely to attract them. Birds also need safe places to nest such as an ivy-clad wall, a large evergreen shrub or dense hedge. Lawns provide food like earthworms, grubs and insects and bog and poolside plantings also attract rich pickings for species like flycatchers.

177

Baby Bird Food

Nestlings, even of seed-eating birds, must be
fed protein-rich insects otherwise they do not
develop properly and may die. This is why you
often see finches apparently pecking at yellow
and white flowers in spring – they are actually
collecting insects drawn to the colour of the
petals. Native hedging, lawns and ponds all
help to attract more insects.

Checklist

▶ **Variety:** Build up mixed borders starting with a structure of small trees, evergreen and deciduous shrubs and climbers.

▶ **Seasonal colour:** Include seasonal highlights to extend border attraction such as berries, autumn leaves, coloured stems, winter and early spring bulbs and blossoms.

▶ **Flowers:** Add long-flowered bush roses, late-flowering clematis, repeat-blooming perennials and bedding.

▶ **Easy care:** Plant herbaceous borders with easy-care equivalents of traditional long-flowering perennials that don't need staking, watering or regular division.

▶ **Mix and match:** Plant in the naturalistic new perennial style using a matrix of ornamental grasses and sedges plus 'prairie-style' flowers.

▶ **Less work:** For low maintenance borders plant mainly evergreen shrubs and ground cover. Use bark mulch to cut down on weeds.

▶ **Cottage garden style:** Combine fragrant, old-fashioned flowering shrubs, perennials, biennials and annuals with attractive fruits, vegetables and herbs.

▶ **Footprint:** Make a feature of productive gardens by giving them an attractive layout

▶ **Ornamental edibles:** Mix pretty fruit and vegetables with edible flowers and herbs and train climbing fruits and vegetables over structures.

▶ **Wildlife:** Attract beneficial insects, birds and other creatures by adapting your garden to create suitable habitats and planting foodstuffs.

179

Pep Up Your Borders

Promoting Flowering

One of the pleasurable outcomes of regularly tending your garden's beds and borders is that plants reward your efforts by looking fresher and flowering for longer. Deadheading is perhaps the most useful activity during the growing season. It brings you in close contact with plants and you will be able to appreciate the intricate flower forms and fragrances as well as notice potential problems. There are different techniques involved in stimulating continued or repeat flower production, but all are straightforward and tailored to achieve optimum results.

Regularly remove faded blooms to extend flowering

Deadheading

Although the novice gardener might consider this a dark art, deadheading is simply the removal of fading blooms that can mar the display of freshly opened flowers or ones still in bud. Also, if you leave the dead petals and yellowing leaves, they are a source of infection. When you deadhead, remove the developing seed head, unless you are growing these for their ornamental value or are collecting fresh seed. You need to do this because plants tend to divert energy to seed production at the expense of flowers.

Annuals

Most annuals decline and die once they have set seed so to keep them blooming all summer long, deadhead regularly with thumb and forefinger, nipping off heads just below the seed pod. For tougher stems, use a pair of kitchen or flower scissors. Don't leave behind long, unbranched flower stems as these turn brown and spoil the overall effect.

Perennials

The displays of most can be extended with regular deadheading using secateurs or flower scissors and the appearance is greatly improved. The following are particularly worth tackling:

► **Delphinium, lupin, verbascum, penstemon and tall campanulas**: cut back the main flower spike at the base, before all the flowers have faded, to just above a side shoot. This encourages smaller, secondary flower shoots to grow.

Lupins

► **Daisy blooms**: e.g. Shasta daisy (Leucanthemum), Osteospermum, Anthemis and Gaillardia.

► **Large individual blooms**: e.g. scabious, peony, daylily, dahlia, bearded iris.

Roses

Use secateurs or flower scissors to snip out faded blooms within a cluster, or individual blooms, on all kinds of roses including climbers. On bush roses, cutting weak-flowering stems back to a strong bud encourages repeat flower flushes as well as making weedy plants fill out more.

183

Hardy herbaceous geraniums flower for weeks

Encouraging Longer Life

Some plants that normally only flower once or twice if left to their own devices, will produce waves of blooms if cut back with shears or secateurs and given a good feed and water to replenish their vigour. Others may or may not flower again but can be rejuvenated and persuaded to produce a new covering of bright, disease-free foliage to help keep the border looking fresh and youthful. Save work by including plenty of ornamental grasses for long-lasting displays through summer into autumn and savour ornamental seed heads, including those produced by shrubs, climbers, perennials and hardy annuals.

Repeat Performance

One of the rules of gardening is that when you cut something back and take away shoots and leaves, you need to provide the plant with enough oomph to get it growing again. After the leafy exuberance promoted by spring rain and warm sunshine, some plants bloom prolifically but then flag. But a quick shear over followed by a drenching and dose of fertilizer often sets them off again. Try this with:

Alchemilla mollis (Lady's mantle)

- ▶ *Creeping campanulas* (some)
- ▶ *Geranium* (cranesbill) (many)
- ▶ *Lamium maculatum* (deadnettle)
- ▶ *Nepeta x faassenii* (catmint)

184

Fresh Leaves

The flower arranger's favourite, Lady's mantle (*Alchemilla mollis*) produces a froth of lime-green flowers over pleated and scalloped leaves but by mid–late summer, seed heads are formed and the leaves lose their lustre. Shearing or strimming to ground level before the seed is released not only saves unwanted seedlings coming up like a rash, but with a good watering and dose of fertilizer, you also get a new crop of leaves, that make an attractive foil for border blooms.

Spot Feeding and Watering

In these environmentally conscious times, it is important to use water in the garden only where necessary and to go about it in the most efficient way possible. This means taking steps to conserve moisture such as applying deep manure mulches in late winter to beds already moist from winter rains. Similarly with fertilizer, you can do more harm than good overfeeding plants or using the wrong mixture.

However well-targeted feeding and watering can really give border displays a lift, especially when gardening on poor and free-draining soils or in areas with low rainfall.

Liquid Feeding and Tonics

Although granular feeds like pelleted chicken manure or fish, blood and bone are ideal for dressing a border prior to planting or at the start of the season to kick-start growth these can take

Comfrey

a while to take effect, especially in a dry spell. Liquid feeds such as dilute comfrey, seaweed or nettle liquor or other organic mixes, get to work straight away. They are especially valuable where plants are starting to flag as the season progresses and need a boost to restore vigour and flower production. Some of these fertilizer tonics can restore leaf colour in sickly plants too, possibly resulting from the lack of a specific nutrient like nitrogen. To restore healthy colouration in hydrangeas that might be suffering an inability to absorb iron, on soil that is too alkaline, treat with sequestered or chelated iron.

Feeding Flowers

Blooms need potassium (chemical symbol K), otherwise known as potash. When plants are shy flowerers it could be down to lack of this nutrient or overfeeding with nitrogen-rich plant food that promotes lush, leafy growth. Try spot feeding with diluted comfrey liquor or liquid tomato feed (both high in potassium).

Targeted Watering

Keep an eye on the weather as an unexpectedly dry spring could cause problems at a critical time in your plants' development. Some winter- and spring-flowering plants suffer if the ground is too dry when the buds have formed e.g. wall-trained camellias often need watering from autumn through to spring to prevent bud drop. In extremely dry summers moisture-lovers like Rudbeckia and Eupatorium might need a few restorative watering cans to prevent wilting.

186

Keeping Up Appearances

Aside from deadheading and weeding, there are all kinds of routine tasks that can help your border stay in tip-top condition, including mulching, dealing with pests early and cutting back over-zealous growth. Where certain pieces of green architecture are supposed to be formal – such as a neatly clipped hedge or topiary figure – regular trimming, so that the contrast between the carefree or 'romantic' and the short cut is sharply defined, is essential. Bulb foliage is a perennial problem for gardeners but there are solutions.

Maintaining Balance

Some plants seem to shoot up and get out of hand the minute you turn your back on them, so casting a critical eye over the border on a fairly regular basis keeps you aware of potential problems in time. Regular spot checks will keep work to a minimum.

Curbing Climbers

A climber's main aim is to follow the light, getting as high as possible by taking the most direct route. But for the best coverage and flowering or fruiting performance, you need to guide the stems towards the horizontal rather than the vertical, regularly tying in shoots to supports and cutting off unwanted growth.

Cotinus
(smoke bush)

187

Fast Foliage

Unlike flowering shrubs, plants grown for their colourful leaves, including certain climbers, can be cut back any time during spring and summer to control over-vigorous growth. Simply trim excess to just above a leaf joint. Plants to watch include:

Ajuga reptans (bugle)

- ▶ *Corylus maxima* 'Purpurea' (purple hazel)
- ▶ *Cotinus* 'Grace' (purple smoke bush)
- ▶ *Humulus lupulus* 'Aureus' (golden hop)
- ▶ *Lonicera nitida* 'Baggesen's Gold' (golden shrubby honeysuckle)
- ▶ *Photinia x fraseri* 'Red Robin'
- ▶ *Physocarpus opulifolius* (gold and purple leaf 'Dart's Gold' and 'Diabolo')
- ▶ *Sambucus* (variegated and gold leaf elder)

Neat Tricks

The following ideas can help give the impression of order even if you haven't got time to do a thorough job:

- ▶ Mow and edge the lawn – it's like vacuuming the carpet!
- ▶ Trim topiary figures and ball-headed standards, cutting off long, wayward shoots.
- ▶ Cut back plants spilling too far over onto paths and patios.

Foliage Fix

Foliage underpins most flowering displays and often, when the blooms are over, the leaves continue to make a show. But leaves can also become unsightly if they run short of water or nutrients, get shredded by pests or succumb to disease. With reasonably swift action though you can remove unsightly leaves and often encourage a completely new set of replacements. You might also be able to grow spectacular foliage displays without fear of damage.

Spring Bulb Makeover

Bulb foliage needs to remain for six to eight weeks after flowering before it can be removed. Don't tie it up in knots! Dying bulb leaves always look rather forlorn but you can minimize the impact on your borders by adopting these two ideas:

▶ **Remove:** Dig up tulip, hyacinth and crown imperial (*Fritillaria imperialis*) clumps once flowers have faded and replant in large plastic tubs or in a spare patch of ground to continue dying down. It helps retrieval if you plant your bulbs in perforated aquatic baskets.

▶ **Replace:** Swap tall daffodils in the border with dwarf types, for example the Cyclamineus group whose foliage is grassier and dies down unobtrusively.

Plant Fritillaria imperialis (crown imperial) in baskets for easy lifting

Top Tip

As spring-flowering hellebores and elephant's ears (*Bergenia*) come into bloom, tidy plants by removing all the old, dead foliage, giving the flowers the perfect backdrop.

Turning a New Leaf

Some spring-flowering woodlander like pulmonaria, *Brunnera macrophylla* and bugle (*Ajuga reptans*) look rather tatty after flowering and in dry weather can succumb to mildew. The best approach is to cut the whole lot down to ground level after flowering, water copiously, mulch and liquid feed to encourage regrowth. The silver-speckled leaves of pulmonaria and white-variegated forms of Brunnera are especially handsome.

189

Hosta Holes

Some plants are like caviare to slugs and snails and so you have to take precautions to ensure they aren't turned into doilies. With hostas the damage is often done when the leaves are still unfurling so do not wait until you see the holes. Try the following approaches:

▶ Pick thick-leaved varieties like 'Halcyon', 'Big Daddy', '
   Sum and Substance' and 'Frances Williams'.
▶ Encircle emerging plants with copper tape.
▶ Sprinkle organic slug pellets.

Mulching

Organic mulches – ones sourced from plants and animals – are an ideal way of maintaining the health and fertility of your soil. They are a boon for plants struggling on poor dry soils or very thin rooty ground under established trees, as they provide a soft, nutritious zone in which roots can proliferate, regardless of what's underneath. Other mulches such as gravel not only look decorative and act as a foil for plants, but also help to keep down weeds and retain moisture, especially when used over a membrane.

Mulching with bark prevents annual weeds

Applying Mulches

Follow these guidelines for effective mulching:

▶ Apply to damp or well-watered ground.
▶ Bark and other organic mulches should be at least 5–7.5 cm (2–3 in) deep, ideally 7.5–10 cm (3–4 in) for manure.

▶ Don't cover plants and keep organic mulch away from the neck or crown.

▶ Replenish bark, cocoa shells etc. before the soil is exposed.

Weed Barrier

Perennial weeds push up through mulches so remove before application. Hoe annual weeds or just smother with the mulch. Mulches prevent light reaching the soil surface stopping weed seeds germinating. This is why they should be topped up if the mulch is disturbed.

Use grass clippings as mulch on shrub borders

Bark Weed Control

Freshly applied ornamental chipped bark gives borders an instant makeover as the dark, even-textured surface provides an ideal foil for plants. It can be expensive to buy bagged so for large areas consider a bulk delivery. Larger-grade bark lasts longer and does not need as frequent application but some mixtures look too coarse for small mixed borders so ask to see a sample.

Mulches for Food and Moisture

Well-rotted, three- to four-year-old manure, garden compost or leaf mould, applied as a thick mulch, seals in moisture, reducing the amount of summer irrigation necessary. It is gradually worked into the soil by worms, improving the structure and releasing valuable nutrients and trace elements.

Top Tip

Sprinkle a general fertilizer like pelleted chicken manure before applying bark as initially it can extract nitrogen from the soil as it starts to rot down.

Alternative Mulches

Try using the following alternatives:

▶ Cocoa shells

▶ Shredded leaves and prunings

▶ Lawn clippings (for shrub borders only)

▶ Gravel and slate chippings

191

Filling Gaps in Borders

At certain times of year borders can look rather threadbare or dull. To improve the look of a bed, after ensuring that plants are given the optimum conditions in which to thrive, you can also add new flowers and foliage. These top-ups might be in the form of garden centre purchases dug in to fill a hole and to create instant impact; bulbs and tubers potted up for planting out later in the season, or seeds sown direct or in pots.

Anemone coronaria

Spring

Many gardens take quite a battering over winter and in a cold spring it can be a while before herbaceous perennials and deciduous shrubs start to green up. At this time of year do not try to fill all the gaps as you'll have a lot more coming through for summer and space rapidly disappears once perennials begin to fill out. Just concentrate on a few areas where the addition of a brightly coloured bulb grouping or early flowering perennial will strengthen the overall look of an existing group of plants.

Potted Bulbs

Nowadays garden centres offer a very wide range of potted bulbs in bud so if you didn't get round to planting any in autumn or you want to boost colour in a particular area, they are a handy resource. Dwarf early flowering bulbs are especially useful for working in between herbaceous plants and low shrubs at the front of the border. For something different in a sunny, sheltered spot try brightly coloured *Anemone coronaria* cultivars or double forms of Persian buttercup (*Ranunculus asiaticus*).

Instant Impact

It's common for nurseries and garden centres to offer certain showy herbaceous perennials and spring shrubs several weeks in advance of them blooming in the garden. Keep an eye on the weather and avoid planting in very cold or windy conditions. Look out for:

- *Chaenomeles* (Japanese quince)
- *Dicentra spectabilis* (bleeding heart)
- Doronicum varieties (leopard's bane)
- *Euphorbia polychroma* (spurge)
- Rhododendrons and azaleas

Dicentra spectabilis (bleeding heart)

Gladioli

Bedding-to-go

Though you normally plant spring bedding in autumn, some of it is also available in spring for instant effect. As well as pansies and violas, you can buy dwarf fragrant wallflowers, hardy primrose and polyanthus.

Planning Ahead

It may seem like a long way in the future but spring is a good time to sow or pot up plants for late summer and autumn

193

enjoyment. If you have a new border, this is an ideal way to fill temporary gaps while you are waiting for shrubs and perennials to grow.

Potting Bulbs for Summer

In spring, garden centres stock a dazzling array of exotic looking bulbs, corms and tubers including flamboyant gladioli and dahlias. Do not be afraid to try something you haven't grown before like the speckled and rainbow-coloured *Tigridia* or curious pineapple lily (*Eucomis bicolor*). Start off under cover while the weather is still cold. Plant out when in bud. Most are tender (lilies are an exception) and need lifting in autumn for storage.

Top Tip

Pot dahlia tubers in 20–25 cm (8–10 in) plastic pots, adding a few centimetres of compost and just covering the tuber initially. Gradually add more compost as the shoots extend. This helps to develop a much larger root system, and bushy growth with more buds.

Cornflowers and corn marigolds

Spring Sowings for Late Blooms

Sow annual black-eyed Susan varieties (*Rudbeckia hirta*) in warmth. Prick out seedlings into individual pots (*see* page 232). These relatively tall daisies blend into mixed and perennial borders with ease, providing colour when most needed from late summer.

Quick-Fill Hardy Annuals

Sow hardy annuals direct in borders to fill gaps. Many bloom eight weeks from sowing.

▶ For continuity sow more every few weeks till early summer.

▶ Between taller perennials and grasses try tall cornfield annuals e.g. cornflower, corn marigold, corncockle.

194

Early Summer Plantings

Long before it's warm enough to plant them (check locally for the last likely frost date in your area), garden centres and DIY stores begin stocking bedding (half-hardy annuals) as well as some potted hardy annuals for instant colour. It pays to make your selections early and if you have frost-free facilities, to pot small plantlets to grow into larger specimens that will have more immediate impact when planted out.

What to Look For

Choose pots and trays of healthy-looking leafy plants not yet in bud or just starting to flower. Plants should be compact. Reject any thin and drawn specimens or those with pale-looking foliage which could indicate trays have been kept too close together or given insufficient light. Threadbare or yellowing foliage suggests pot-bound plants or irregular watering.

Half-hardy Bedding

Bedding comes in a range of sizes and shades. Single colours are easier to work into existing schemes. Short varieties are ideal for gap filling towards the front of a border or in raised beds but some medium to tall varieties blend happily with perennials. Good plants to try in this situation include:

▶ *Agastache* 'Blue Fortune'
▶ *Antirrhinum majus* varieties (snapdragon)
▶ *Brachyscome iberidifolia* (Swan river daisy)
▶ *Cosmos bipinnatus* Sonata Series
▶ *Nicotiana* alata 'Limelight' (tobacco plant)
▶ *Salvia coccinea* 'Lady in Red'

Brachyscome iberidifolia (Swan river daisy)

195

Annual Climbers

For height in borders grow hardy annual sweet peas (*Lathyrus odoratus*) or canary creeper (*Tropaeolum peregrinum*) up cane wigwams, or try more exotic looking half-hardy vines like Spanish flag (*Ipomoea lobata*) and black-eyed Susan (*Thunbergia alata* 'African Sunset').

Late Summer Additions

By mid summer and the onset of warm nights, more sub-tropical-looking plants and larger specimens begin to come in to the garden centres. These have usually been hardened off and so can go straight out into the border. Larger plants are expensive but being more strident and colourful, you only need one or two to make a statement.

Thunbergia alata (African Sunset)

Summer Bulbs and Tubers

During high summer place the potted up bulbs and tubers planted in spring into gaps in the mixed border. You can also find plenty of lush flowering and foliage plants on sale. Treat yourself to a specimen-size dark-leaf dahlia, a snowy-white summer hyacinth (*Galtonia candicans*), or a large pot of blue agapanthus. 'Plunge' in a bed (leaving the pot in place) to make autumn lifting easier, or plant normally.

Agapanthus

196

Tender Perennials

These plants work just as well in borders as they do in patio pots and certain types make superb instant gap fillers in a mixed border. Pelargoniums perform well in dry ground but you'll need more moisture for the other classics, bedding fuchsias and Marguerite daisies (*Argyranthemum*). Also try:

- ▶ *Begonia* 'Bonfire'
- ▶ *Diascia* cultivars
- ▶ *Fuchsia* 'Thalia'
- ▶ *Heliotropium* (heliotrope)
- ▶ *Nemesia* Maritana Series
- ▶ *Osteospermum*
- ▶ *Verbena* 'Homestead Purple'

Red or purple cordyline add a sub-tropical feel

Foliage Exotica

Large leafy plants create a focal point when surrounded by fine-textured flowers and foliage. Consider a tree fern (*Dicksonia*), a stripy-leaved Indian shot like *Canna* 'Tropicanna', a banana lookalike; or a red or purple-leaf cabbage palm (*Cordyline australis*). Closer to ground level grow purple, lime-green or variegated coleus (*Solenostemon*).

Autumn

As summer fades into autumn and the nights grow colder, most annual flowers begin to look a little jaded. However, deciduous shrubs with their developing tints and the red, orange and gold blooms of late perennials really come into their own and just need a few extras to create some really eye-catching displays.

197

Calluna vulgaris (heather)

Bulbs

Plant hardy potted cyclamen (*Cyclamen hederifolium*) under trees and also plant dry bulbs of autumn crocus species and Colchicum as soon as they come into the shops. They bloom in record time.

Bedding

Look out for bright ornamental peppers and chillies and winter cherry (*Solanum* 'Thurino'). These won't survive frosts but along with dwarf chrysanthemums add colour in raised beds round the patio. Pansies and violas last well into winter.

Solanum 'Thurino' (winter cherry)

Late Shrubs and Perennials

Dwarf asters in rich blues and purples combine beautifully with autumn colours. Plant in the foreground along with smouldering heathers (*Calluna vulgaris*), which require acid soil. Drop taller perennials including *Anemone x hybrida* and specimen-sized flowering ornamental grasses such as Pennisetum in between shrubs. Hydrangeas are also good buys for instant drama.

198

Checklist

▶ **Flower power:** Deadhead roses, perennial and annual blooms where practical. Cut back main flower spires of plants like delphinium to encourage secondary spikes.

▶ **Trim:** Shear over spring carpeters and *Alchemilla mollis*, to encourage fresh foliage.

▶ **Pep up:** Cut back certain summer-blooming herbaceous after each flush to encourage repeating. Feed and water to encourage regrowth after cutting back.

▶ **Ornamental seeds:** Leave certain flowers to develop attractive seed pods.

▶ **Remedies:** Treat plants suffering nutrient deficiencies with appropriate tonics.

▶ **Boost growth:** Encourage shy-flowering plants using potassium-rich feeds, watering and mulching.

▶ **Keep control:** Cut back over-vigorous growth on foliage shrubs and climbers.

▶ **Makeover:** Create a makeover illusion by mowing, trimming topiary and tidying sprawling edges. Remove bulbs with unsightly foliage to die back behind the scenes.

▶ **Spring Perennials:** Tidy foliage before evergreens bloom.

▶ **Mulching:** Use bark to reduce weeding and thick organic mulches to conserve moisture and feed plants.

▶ **Pot and sow:** Pot up summer-flowering bulbs and tubers in spring and sow late- flowering hardy annuals to add summer/autumn colour.

▶ **Colour burst:** Sow quick-flowering hardy annuals, plant bulbs, seasonal bedding and eye-catching specimens to boost borders.

199

Basic Upkeep

Routine Tasks

Once everything is planted, you will need to find out how best to look after your beds and borders. Shrub borders need very little work, especially if they are mulched to control weeds. Mixed beds have a number of peaks in activity with some jobs like dividing perennials and pruning done once a year or every two years while others, like deadheading, as often as once a week in summer.

Wear gloves when handling fertilizers

Feeding

Replenishing lost nutrients is an essential part of border maintenance and there are a number of ways of maintaining fertility and giving plants what they need at key points in the season. You'll find a bewildering array of chemical fertilizers in garden centres and home improvement stores as well as an increasing number of organic products. Fertilizers come as dry powders and granules, as well as liquid formulations.

Fertilizer Dressings

Always follow packet instructions and do not overfeed as this can cause too much soft, juicy growth which is attractive to sap-sucking pests, fungal diseases and wind damage. Slow-release fertilizers emit a steady supply of nutrients, increasing with rising temperatures and moisture levels when plants are growing more quickly. They only need to be applied once or twice a year. General fertilizers are applied as follows:

▶ **Base dressing:** Raked into soil surface prior to sowing or planting.

▶ **Top dressing:** Worked in around growing and established plants.

Liquids and Tonics

Dilute liquid fertilizers according to instructions and water on to roots or spray leaves as a foliar feed. Some liquid fertilizers are used as tonics for plants with poor growth or ones showing nutrient deficiencies. For example seaweed-based tonics containing chelated or sequestered iron and other trace elements, are used to counteract lime-induced chlorosis (yellowing of leaves due to inability to absorb iron and other micro-nutrients).

Organic Options

Maintaining soil fertility is crucial to organic gardening and garden compost, mulches and home-made fertilizers play an important part. If yours is a tiny urban plot and you do not have storage room, you can buy organic liquid concentrate and granular fertilizers and fit a slimline plastic compost bin.

Bulky Organics

Though not strictly organic if the original material didn't come from an organic source, most gardeners are happy to compromise and use three-year-old manure, seaweed, recycled waste produced by a digester or their own garden compost to provide bulky organic matter for border soils. These products:

203

▶ Supply at least some of the nitrogen, phosphorus and potassium required as well as micro-nutrients.

▶ Improve the physical qualities of the soil, developing a crumb structure in clay and increasing moisture-holding capacity in free-draining soils.

▶ Help maintain a healthy flora and fauna.

Applying Mulches

There are a few points to consider when applying mulches:

▶ Only apply to damp soil. Late winter is ideal.

▶ Do not put on too soon – winter rains can wash out nutrients like nitrogen before plants can absorb them.

▶ Do not pile up round the base or neck of plants.

▶ Put on thickly – at least 7.5–10 cm (3–4 in).

▶ Do not apply at the same time as lime.

Making Comfrey Fertilizer

Russian comfrey (*Symphytum x uplandicum*) is a vigorous herbaceous plant with blue spring flowers, attractive to bees. 'Bocking 14' doesn't set seed. Grow in a spare sunny

Top Tip

Bush roses are gross feeders and need a rich diet. Mulch with copious quantities of manure or garden compost in late winter (this supplies many of the required micro-nutrients such as boron and manganese, as well as kick-starting new shoot growth with nitrogen). Bury black bananas or skins next to bushes to supply additional potassium. On poor soils use additional granular rose feed.

Top Tip

If manure or compost does not get hot enough, weed seeds survive and can cause problems sprouting from mulches.

spot for a year to harvest the following year. Produce ready-to-use, potassium-rich fertilizer by quartrer-filling a container with leaves and topping up with water (wait 3–5 weeks before use) or make concentrate. Then do the following:

▶ Drill a ¾ inch hole in the base of a barrel or large plastic container or fit with a tap.

▶ Raise the barrel up on bricks.

▶ Put bottle under hole.

▶ Fill with leaves and fit a lid with weights to put pressure on the foliage.

▶ After 2–3 weeks begin to collect the thick brown liquor and store in a cool dark place.

▶ Dilute 10 to 15 parts water to one of comfrey liquor and water regularly.

Weeding

Weeds are unwanted plants that compete for nutrients, space and light with plants you do want to grow. Some cultivated varieties can become weeds in the border if they seed too prolifically or have a running root system. Equally, quite a few wild species are actually quite attractive in borders or are worth keeping on the garden's margins to provide food for beneficial insects.

205

Weeds compete for water and nutrients

Hand Weeding

Most weeds can be dealt with either by pulling them out or easing out with a hand or border fork.

▶ Pull weeds when the soil is damp as they come out more easily.

▶ Remove weeds when small and before they get entrenched with a big root system.

▶ Pull fast-spreading annual weeds before they flower and set seed.

▶ Shake off as much soil from the roots as possible.

Hoeing

When the soil surface is dry, preferably on a windy or sunny day, hoe between plants with a long-handled Dutch hoe. Keep the scuffling action shallow so as not to disturb the soil structure or bring more weed seeds to the surface. Leave uprooted weeds on the

Top Tip

Do not put the seed heads of weeds or border perennials like lady's mantle (*Alchemilla mollis*) in the compost bin. They might survive and cause a weed nuisance when the compost is spread.

206

Top Tip

Hoeing is only suitable for controlling annual weeds which die when the top is severed from the roots or seedlings are uprooted. Perennial weeds can proliferate if chopped into pieces by a hoe, as both stem and root fragments can grow back.

surface to wither. Use a handheld hoe in small gaps between plants.

Mulching

Minimizing soil disturbance and excluding light from the soil surface stops new weed seeds germinating. A good way to do this, especially between shrubs and ground cover plants where you aren't planting seasonally, is by covering the ground with a good depth of bark chippings or shredded prunings which take a long time to rot down. Top up thin patches routinely. Initially fungi extract nitrogen from the soil to start the rotting process so before adding bark or coco shell mulch, apply a dressing of pelleted chicken manure.

Problem Weeds

Perennial weeds are difficult to eradicate as you only need to leave a little bit of root in the ground and they grow back. Bindweed, creeping thistle, dandelion, creeping buttercup, bramble, couch grass (switch), ground elder and horsetail or mare's tail (*Equisetum*) are among the worst offenders.

Manual Weeding

Provided you can get all the roots out, some perennials can be vanquished by repeated digging. This is not always so straightforward in a border full of herbaceous perennials since the weed systems can become intertwined. Weeds with running roots like ground elder and couch grass can travel over long distances.

Top Tip

You cannot compost perennial weeds so instead of throwing them away in the rubbish, make fertilizer out of them (use the same method for making dilute comfrey as on page 205). Nettle 'tea' is a good free source of nitrogen. Put leftover sludge on the compost heap.

Glyphosate-based Weedkiller

This chemical does not harm beneficial invertebrates (mini-beasts) or bees if used according to instruction. Sprayed or painted on to actively growing weed leaves, the chemical spreads through and kills the root system.

Pest and Disease Control

To catch problems at the outset, make regular inspections of shoot tips and flower buds, turning over leaves and using a hand-held magnifier if necessary. Keep plants growing strongly to maintain their immunity.

Dealing with Common Pests

Hand picking or rubbing off with thumb and forefinger is a
quick and easy chemical free solution. Wear latex gloves if
you're squeamish.

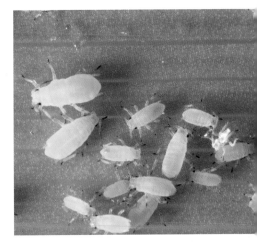

- ▶ **Aphids:** Also called greenfly. They can be black, pink,
  grey or covered in white wool. Sap suckers concentrate
  on shoot tips and buds. Snip off affected shoots or rub
  away colonies.

- ▶ **Slugs and snails:** Produce ragged holes and silvery slime
  trails. Patrol at night with a torch to catch them in the
  open and put water on parasitic slug nematodes.

Aphids (greenfly) give birth to live young

- ▶ **Caterpillars:** Often camouflaged and can quickly skeletonize leaves. Hand pick caterpillars and rub
  off eggs. Wear gloves as some have irritant hairs.

- ▶ **Vine weevil:** Creamy U-shaped grubs with brown heads. Devastate whole root systems causing sudden
  plant collapse. Adults leave U-shaped holes in evergreen foliage. Treat with vine weevil nematodes.

Encouraging Natural Predators

There is a time delay between an explosion of insect pests like aphids and the appearance of their
natural predators so don't immediately reach for the insecticide spray as newly emerging predators
won't have anything to eat.

Ladybird adults and larvae eat aphids

The Good Guys

There are all kinds of beneficial creatures including parasitic and predatory wasps but some are particularly useful for controlling pests:

▶ **Hoverfly:** Striped in appearance, mimicking bees and wasps. Adults attracted to simple white, yellow and orange flowers. Larvae eat aphids.

▶ **Ladybird:** Adults are often red with black spots. Help to overwinter by leaving borders uncut till spring. Larvae have voracious appetite for aphids.

▶ **Lacewing:** Brown or green boggle-eyed insects with long lacy wings. Larvae feed on aphids etc. Adults need nectar plants.

▶ **Ground beetle:** Fast-moving black or iridescent beetles which prey on slugs and grubs. Love ground-cover plants and bark mulch.

Amphibians and Birds

Encourage insect- and grub-eating birds with food, nest boxes and shelter planting. Slug-eating amphibians need damp areas, log or rock piles and long grass.

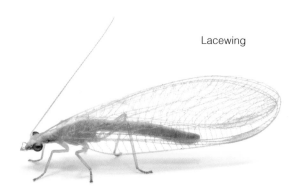

Lacewing

Dealing with Disease

Plants generally suffer from diseases when they aren't growing in ideal circumstances and are stressed as a consequence. For example trees and shrubs in waterlogged soil could succumb to root rot or phytopthora. Overcrowding and overfeeding should also be avoided. Pick off affected leaves and shoots at first sign and prune out dead or damaged wood.

Common Fungal Problems

Watch out for the following:

▶ **Grey mould:** Common in autumn and spring with cold temperatures and low light levels. Grey furry coating on yellowing leaves and flower buds. Pick off dead material and yellowing leaves regularly.

▶ **Powdery mildew:** White powdery coating on leaves and stems, common during drought. Cut back, water, mulch and liquid feed to stimulate re-growth.

▶ **Coral spot:** Bright coral-coloured raised spots, mostly on dead wood but can infect living material. Prune out dead parts promptly.

▶ **Black spot:** On rose leaves – yellowing with black spots and early leaf fall. Black sunken lesions on affected stems. Grow resistant varieties. Pick up and destroy all leaf debris and prune out affected stems.

Black spot

211

Pruning Shrubs and Climbers

Pruning deciduous shrubs and climbers helps to improve bloom quality and size and keep them productive. Meanwhile, pruning foliage varieties often makes the leaves larger and brighter. By cutting back certain stems you can change the shape and size of a plant or improve its appearance. Pruning also helps to control disease, partly by allowing in more light and increasing air circulation.

Kerria

When and How to Prune

Use a pair of good quality secateurs and for thicker stems, loppers or a small, fold-away pruning saw. A heavy-duty pruning saw or bow saw might occasionally be needed for thick branches. Aside from avoiding frosty periods, when you prune is very important. A rule of thumb is that anything blooming before the longest day is pruned lightly, post blooming. Plants flowering after the longest day (with the exception of *Hydrangea macrophylla*) are pruned hard in spring.

Early Shrubs

This group includes deciduous spring-flowering forsythia, flowering currant (*Ribes*) and *Kerria* and early summer bloomers such as mock orange (*Philadelphus*), weigela and deutzia. All produce flowers on the previous season's wood so prune immediately after flowering to give re-growth chance to mature. Remember to also:

▶ Remove any dead or damaged wood and crossing branches.

▶ Reduce flowered stems back to a strong side shoot.

▶ To keep shrubs youthful, take out about one in five of the oldest stems close to base.

▶ On suckering shrubs like *Kerria*, cut back flowered shoots to near the base, just above a strong non-flowering side shoot.

Late Shrubs

Late shrubs flower on new wood (current season's growth) so can be pruned back to a low framework of branches in spring. This group includes most deciduous foliage and coloured-stemmed shrubs and late bloomers like buddleia, hardy fuchsia, *Hydrangea paniculata*, *Caryopteris x clandonensis* and bush roses.

Long-flowering Shrubs

Potentilla fruticosa and *Hypericum* 'Hidcote' bloom over a long period on new shoot tip growths. To keep youthful, cut out a third of the oldest stems on established plants. Mophead and lacecap *Hydrangea macrophylla* cultivars bloom on the previous

Prune *Hydrangea macrophylla* (mopheads and lacecaps) only very lightly

Prune shrub roses lightly, removing dead stems

season's wood even though they are relatively late blooming. Leave old flower heads on over winter to protect new flower buds. In mid spring, cut stems back to a pair of strong buds a little way back from shoot tips.

Pruning Roses

Only prune roses very lightly in their first year. Cut out dead, diseased or damaged wood on all roses and thin bush roses to create an open framework of branches.

Shrub and Bush Roses

▶ **Bush roses:** These include hybrid tea or large-flowered, and floribunda or cluster-flowered. They are prolific, blooming on wood produced in the current year. Along with compact patio roses, they should be hard pruned by ½ to ¾ in late winter. Also remove a proportion of the oldest wood.

▶ **Shrub roses:** Once-flowering kinds are only reduced in branch length by about a third at the most with virtually no thinning.

▶ **English roses:** Cut these repeat-flowering shrubs to between a third and a half, creating a rounded profile.

214

Climbers and Ramblers

▶ **Modern repeat-flowering climbers:** Cut flowering stems back to about 3–4 buds from their origin, creating short spurs. These produce next year's flowering shoots.

▶ **Ramblers:** These are very vigorous. Tie the new growth made after early summer blooming into supports in autumn while still flexible. Take out some of the oldest wood if necessary.

Pruning Evergreens

Evergreen shrubs are generally pruned in late spring and early summer, so that any vulnerable new shoots generated won't be caught by late frosts. If you clip topiary several times in the season, make the last cut late summer, giving re-growth chance to toughen up before winter. Shear English lavender after flowering to keep plants bushy. Cut off about 2.5 cm (1 in) of shoot tips.

Dealing with Frost Damage

Mild winter weather often promotes a flush of new leaf growth that gets frosted in spring. Californian lilac (*Ceanothus*) also frequently suffers die-back through cold winters. Wait until early to mid summer before cutting out damage, as shoots with blackened leaves frequently re-sprout.

Shear over English lavendar after flowering or in spring before they begin growing

Silver Herbs

To prevent legginess, cut cotton lavender (*Santolina*), Artemisia 'Powis Castle' and curry plant (*Helichrysum italicum*) back hard to signs of re-growth in the bottom third of stems.

215

Pruning Bamboos

Enhance tall clump-forming bamboos by pruning three-year and older plants as follows:

▶ Clear all side shoots from bottom third of stems.
▶ Remove thin growths at ground level.
▶ Thin out a proportion of oldest stems to allow light through.

Clematis

Pruning Climbers

Though the growth habit of climbers seems quite different from that of shrubs, the same general rule applies regarding when to prune, with a few exceptions. You can see this quite clearly with clematis. Those flowering early are pruned after flowering and only very lightly, if at all. If you pruned them hard in spring, you'd remove all the potential flowers! Ones flowering after the longest day, through late summer and autumn, can be pruned hard in late winter and will still have long enough to produce sufficiently mature flowering wood.

Clematis Pruning Groups

Early flowering clematis need only very light pruning

Clematis are divided into numbered pruning groups as follows:

▶ **Group 1:** Winter and spring flowering, blooming on previous season's growth e.g. *Clematis cirrhosa* forms, *C. alpina* and *C. macropetalla* cultivars, *C. montana* and *C. armandii*. Prune very lightly, mid to late spring after frosts, but only to cut back over-long shoots and dead stems.

216

▶ **Group 2:** Early large-flowered hybrids blooming on short growths arising from previous year's wood. Trim dead shoot ends back to a pair of large buds in late winter/early spring. Also prune lightly after first flowering in early summer, cutting back to large buds a little below flowers to encourage side shoots which should bear a late-summer crop of blooms.

▶ **Group 3:** Late-flowering clematis blooming on current season's growth e.g. Viticella and Texensis hybrids, late, large-flowered hybrids and *C. tangutica* and *C. orientalis* cultivars. Prune late winter, taking plants down to between 30 and 90 cm (1–3 ft from ground level), cutting just above a strong pair of buds. Or prune as for Group 2 to maintain a larger area of cover.

Pruning Wisteria

Wisteria are incredibly vigorous and need pruning twice a year, both to curb their growth and encourage flowering wood which produces the pendulous blooms from late spring. Prune as follows:

▶ **Late summer:** Reduce the length of long whip-like growths to 5–6 leaves. This helps develop flowering spurs (short side shoots). Maintain a framework of stems, tying securely to wires to cover required area.

▶ **Late winter:** Further reduce the same growths to 2–3 buds.

Wisteria

Other Climbers

Prune common honeysuckle (*Lonicera pericymenum*) by about a third once they've bloomed and prune climbing hydrangea (*Hydrangea anomala subsp. petiolaris*) after flowering, to curb over-vigorous shoots.

217

Caring for Perennials

Herbaceous perennials are generally tough and easy to care for. If anything, their vigour is what causes demands on maintenance such as lifting and dividing, regular feeding and staking. Evergreen types may suffer in cold winters. Perennials and bulbs are well worth the extra effort involved to keep them in tip top shape as they contribute so much colour and interest in the border.

Regular Jobs

Throughout winter, herbaceous plants sit dormant, their faded top growth helping to insulate the roots and provide cover for insects and other creatures. When the weather warms up in spring and new shoots start to appear, it's time for action. Routine jobs done well then, such as staking (*see* page 73), pay dividends throughout the summer.

Lifting and Dividing

Quick-growing, floriferous perennials tend to run out of steam after a couple of years. You will see the congested centre dying off with young fresh growth round the outside. Some perennials won't need dividing for several years so wait till you begin to see the tell-tale signs. Divide late summer and autumn perennials in spring, and spring and early summer types in autumn (*see* page 234).

Lupins, oriental poppy and perennial cornflower

Bulbs

Once flowering of plants like daffodils begins to decline and there aren't any obvious signs of disease, lift clumps just after flowering and split congested bulbs. Replenish soil and replant.

Cutting Back Perennials

Tidy up perennials as follows:

▶ **Herbaceous:** Clear collapsed remains if covering evergreen shrubs, herbs and groundcover. Prune or pull away overwintered stems of most in spring once new growth is detected.

▶ **Penstemon:** In mid spring, cut back top growth to just above where the stems are sprouting.

Penstemon (beard-tongue)

▶ **Grasses and evergreen foliage:** Cut back deciduous grass clumps to just above where you see new shoots appearing in spring. Tidy evergreen grasses by combing out dead leaves and pick off dead or damaged leaves on foliage perennials like *Heuchera*.

Feeding Perennials and Bulbs

Apply a top dressing of general fertilizer e.g. fish, blood and bone or pelleted chicken manure around perennial plants in spring. A late-winter mulch (*see* page 204) helps conserve moisture. Feed spring bulbs with a potassium-rich liquid fertilizer immediately after flowering.

219

Winter Protection

Some plants are borderline hardy and, particularly in colder regions, you take a risk leaving them in beds over winter without extra insulation. Some evergreen shrubs and topiary plants may be generally hardy but susceptible to winter damage from cold, drying winds. If you have frost-free shelter such as a garage or conservatory, many vulnerable or tender plants can be brought indoors in autumn. Others must be protected where they stand.

Indoors and Out

Although it creates more work, gardeners use many different tender perennial flowering and foliage plants to boost border colour and foliage interest. Indoor or conservatory plants can also be 'plunged' in borders during the summer for temporary effect.

Tender Bulbs and Tubers

If your garden is too cold for plants to be left in the ground and protected in situ, lift and store as follows:

▶ **Corms and tubers:** After the first frost has blackened foliage, lift corms and tubers carefully to avoid damaging roots as this introduces disease. Cut off top growth.

Gladioli
corms

▶ **Gladioli and freesia:** Allow corms to dry off and then remove old corm and small bulbils. Store in a dark, frost-free place covering with dry, soil-less compost or sand.

▶ **Canna and dahlia:** Wash soil from the tubers, discard any rotten sections and leave to dry off. Upturn dahlia tubers to allow moisture to drain from cut stem bases (2–3 weeks). Cover tubers within sand or potting compost, leaving remains of flower stems exposed.

House and Conservatory Plants

Bring indoors in early autumn as the nights begin to get cooler but before any danger of frost. Check for signs of pests.

Fuchsias and Other Tender Perennials

Lift and store the mother plant in a light, cool but frost-free place or take cuttings in late summer or early autumn. The latter take up far less room and in spring are potted up and grown on. Store tender fuchsias as follows:

▶ Wait until the foliage is falling naturally, lift and cut back stems by two thirds. Pick off remaining leaves.

▶ Allow soil on roots to dry out substantially. Pack tightly together in cool, dark place e.g. a newspaper-lined cardboard box in the garage.

Tender fuchsias
need frost-free
protection

Phormium
(New Zealand flax)

Protecting in Situ

It can be impractical to lift and store large plants under cover for winter and so vulnerable specimens need to be protected where they stand. It pays to have a supply of horticultural fleece handy for draping over plants like mop head hydrangeas and pieris when late spring frosts are forecast.

Wrapping Tender Plants

Use the following methods:

▶ Fit insulating pipe lagging to protect stems of standard topiary from frost penetration. Wrap heads of bay, box and *Ligustrum* with fleece.

▶ Use fleece and hessian, packed with straw and bracken, to insulatetender shrubs, tree ferns and hardy banana (*Musa basjoo*).

Root Protection

In areas experiencing mild winters, especially on free-draining soil, you can often get away with leaving tender bulbs, corms and tubers like gladioli and dahlia in the border. Cover the ground with a mound of bark chippings to prevent frost penetration. Also protect other borderline hardy perennials such as *Melianthus major*, agapanthus and penstemons in the same way (keep bark from base of woody shoots) as well as coloured and variegated New Zealand flax (*Phormium*) and tender shrubs (see above).

222

Checklist

▶ **Fertilizer and compost:** Apply a fertilizer dressing in spring and use rose fertilizer around roses on poor soil. Mulch borders with bulky organics in late winter.

▶ **Potassium:** Feed to enhance flowering, fruiting and hardiness using home-made comfrey fertilizer. Treat spring bulbs immediately after blooming.

▶ **Weeding:** Pull annual weeds when soil is damp and hoe when dry. Mulch shrub borders with bark etc. to minimize weeding. Dig out problem weeds or spray off with glyphosate-based weedkiller.

▶ **Pests:** Remove pests by hand or use biological control. Encourage natural predators.

▶ **Plant health:** Maintain healthy growing conditions to minimize disease. Cut out affected parts, collect up fallen infected leaves and prune.

▶ **Early/late prunning:** Lightly prune early flowering shrubs/climbers blooming on the previous season's wood after flowering. Prune wisteria late summer and late winter.

▶ **Longest day:** Hard prune shrubs, bush and patio roses and clematis blooming after the longest day, mostly in late winter (NOT *Hydrangea macrophylla*).

▶ **Roses:** Prune English and shrub roses relatively lightly.

▶ **Evergreens:** Prune evergreens, removing frost damage, early to mid summer.

▶ **Spring makeover:** Cut back perennials and divide once new growth detected.

▶ **Tender care:** Lift and store tender bulbs, tubers and tender perennials in autumn. Protect large, frost-sensitive plants in situ.

Propagation

Raising Plants from Seed

This can be a most rewarding and economic gardening activity. You will probably see a lot more variation in colour, height and flower form than in bought seed and it is exciting waiting to see what comes up. Fresh seed often germinates faster too. Most hardy annual and biennial flowers are easy to grow, but good results also come from common bedding varieties and many cottage garden perennials.

Collecting Seed

Not all flowers collected from the garden will come true from seed due to cross-pollination and this is particularly the case with seed collected from F1 varieties but do not let that put you off. Follow these instructions for collecting:

▶ **Harvesting:** Collect seeds in dry, sunny conditions.

▶ **Selecting:** Look for swollen seed pods that have changed from green to brown or plants with dry, shrivelled flowers like French marigold.

▶ **Cuttting:** Carefully cut stems bearing numerous pods or nip off individual heads. Upturn stems into separate, labelled paper bags.

Top Tip

Where flower colours are mixed or a shade varies, select your favourites and label with coloured wool or twine as a reminder which plants to collect from. Deadhead the others before they drop seed, and only sow collected seed, to create your ideal strain.

▶ **Drying out:** Leave to dry in a cool airy place for a few days before separating seed.

▶ **Preparing to store:** Roll pods between fingers or crush lightly with a rolling pin to release the ripe brown or black seed. Store in labelled envelopes in a cool place; a metal can with lid or other rodent-safe container is ideal.

Good Choices

The following collection of annual, biennial and perennial flowers and herbs usually produce good results when sown.

▶ *Borago officinalis* (borage)
▶ *Calendula officinalis* (pot marigold)
▶ *Campanula percisifolia* (bellflower)
▶ *Cosmos bippinatus* (cosmos)

▶ *Digitalis purpurea* including '*Excelsior Hybrids*' (foxglove)
▶ Geum 'Mrs J. Bradshaw' and 'Lady Strathedon'
▶ *Helianthus annuus* (sunflower)
▶ *Lathyrus odoratus* (sweet pea)
▶ *Lavandula angustifolia* (English lavender)
▶ *Lunaria annua* (honesty)
▶ *Lychnis coronaria* (dusty miller)
▶ *Nigella damascena* (love-in-a-mist)
▶ *Papaver rhoeas* (field poppy/Shirley poppy)
▶ *Papaver somniferum* (opium poppy)
▶ *Tagetes patula* (French marigold)
▶ *Tropaeolum majus* (nasturtium)
▶ *Verbena bonariensis*

Sowing Outdoors

You can grow quite a lot of flowers from seed without any special facilities such as a greenhouse and direct-sown seedlings require less maintenance. Most hardy annual varieties work well and if you sow quick-maturing types every few weeks between early spring and early summer, you can have a succession of fresh blooms.

Soil Preparation

In spring, wait until the soil surface has dried out and you can work it into a fine tilth with a rake. To do this, break down any large clods and move the rake forwards and backwards, levelling out the patch of ground and making a fine, crumb-like surface to sow into.

Natural Effects

Hardy annuals and cornfield varieties tend to look best in natural-looking swathes and when woven through other plants. You can achieve this by:

▶ **Broadcasting or sprinkling seed:** Do this on the soil surface to mimic natural dispersal. Ideal for seed freshly collected from plants including biennials like foxglove, forget-me-not and honesty as well as freely germinating perennials such as *Verbena bonariensis*, dusty miller (*Lychnis coronaria*) and peach-leaved bellflower (*Campanula percisifolia*).

Top Tip

Sow biennials in trays of compost or in rows in a spare patch of ground in early summer, and move plants to their final positions (when large enough to handle) to flower the following spring or summer.

▶ **Sowing in patches:** This gives more controlled results. Mark out various organic shapes to sow separate varieties into, but within these patches, sow in straight lines (see packet instructions for sowing depth). This allows you to spot and remove weed seedlings.

Thinning Seedlings

Sow as thinly as possible but where seedlings do come up too thickly, it's best to pull out a few to let the strongest grow without competition. If you leave them all crowded together they will become tall and lanky and more prone to disease. Push in twiggy stick to support taller annuals support.

After-care

Don't be caught out by dry spells. Use a fine rose on a watering can to water sown areas, encouraging germination and keeping vulnerable seedlings moist until established.

Sowing Indoors

Seed from half-hardy annuals and other tender plants needs warmth and humidity to trigger germination but most then tolerate or prefer cooler conditions in which to grow on. Most of us have room to start off a few seeds on a warm, light window ledge and should be able to grow them to the planting out stage without special facilities. However, a greenhouse or conservatory is useful, because as the seedlings are pricked out and potted on, they inevitably take up a lot more space.

229

Using a Propagator

An electric propagator (preferably with a thermostat) will maintain the correct temperature range for germination (see seed packet). But if you don't want to go to that expense, either buy an unheated windowsill propagator with a clear vented lid, or simply cover seed trays or pots with clingfilm, a clear plastic bag or piece of glass. This covering creates a greenhouse effect that maintains warmth and humidity.

Top Tip

To avoid disturbing the seed, stand trays and pots in a shallow container of water and allow the compost to soak it up. Remove once the surface has gone dark and cover to maintain humidity or place in a propagator.

Light or Dark

Most seed isn't fussy either way but some types are particular. Especially with very fine seed, a few require light for germination. Simply press seed into the compost surface. With busy Lizzie you can lightly sprinkle over the sown seed with vermiculite which allows light to penetrate.

Light-requiring types include:

- ▶ *Antirrhinum* (snapdragon)
- ▶ *Begonia*
- ▶ *Impatiens* (busy Lizzie)
- ▶ *Nicotiana* (tobacco plant)
- ▶ *Petunia*

Impatiens (busy Lizzie)

With plants that need
darkness, cover with a black
plastic refuse bag and check
regularly. Remove the cover as
soon as germination is spotted.
Dark-loving plants include:

▶ *Calendula officinalis* (pot marigold)
▶ Delphinium
▶ *Nemesia*
▶ *Viola* (pansy)

Preparation and Sowing

Fill scrupulously clean seed trays or pots with seed and cutting
compost, breaking up any larger lumps with your fingers. Use a flat
piece of wood or similar to gently firm the compost to leave a smooth
surface. Sow as thinly as possible and cover with sieved compost to
required depth (or leave uncovered – *see* page 230)

Growing Seedlings On

Once seeds have germinated, which usually takes between a few days and a couple of weeks,
success or failure depends on how you grow the seedlings on and how you ready the plantlets for life
outdoors. Very early spring sowings produce seedlings that need looking after for longer, since tender
plants cannot be planted out before the last likely frost date. Later sowings often catch up with earlier
ones because of the higher light levels.

Pricking Out

Once seedlings are large enough to handle, usually after the first true leaves have appeared, prick out the strongest. If the seedling leaves (cotyledons) are large, as in sunflowers, prick out immediately. Space at least 3.8 cm (1½ in) apart or use individual pots.

▶ **Roots:** Holding a leaf gently, use a pencil to lift the roots out with as much compost as possible.

▶ **Compost:** Make a hole in a pot or tray of compost to accommodate the roots and gently firm in.

▶ **Take care:** Don't hold delicate seedlings by the roots or stem.

▶ **Watering:** Settle compost round the transplanted seedlings using a watering can with a fine rose head.

Ideal Conditions

Maintain the following conditions for optimal growth and to avoid damping off disease (a fungal infection that causes seedlings to collapse):

232

Top Tip

If growing a variety with mixed colours, prick out a range of seedling sizes and leaf shades to get as wide a range as possible.

▶ **Increase ventilation:** Gradually once germination occurs, eventually removing the cover altogether. Turn the thermostat down on electric propagators and gradually open up the vents.

▶ **Maintain moisture levels:** Use a hand sprayer to dampen compost.

▶ **Provide even light:** Place seedlings in good light, but not strong sunshine which could cause scorching. Turn plants regularly to keep growth upright.

▶ **Avoid fungal problems:** Supply good light and increased ventilation after germination and use tap water only.

Hardening Off

A couple of weeks before it is safe to plant out, begin to acclimatize plantlets to outdoor conditions. Stand in a sheltered spot out of direct sun for a couple of hours to begin with and gradually increase time. Liquid feed or pot on plantlets if they show signs of starvation.

233

Easy Propagation

Vegetative propagation (rooting divisions and cuttings) ensures that the offspring are identical to the parent. Most herbaceous perennials are easy to bulk up by taking advantage of the way they grow naturally. As divisions and other propagated parts are fairly mature compared to seedlings, they tend to establish readily. You do not need special equipment, although potting plant sections up and growing on in a greenhouse or cold frame for a few weeks can be a speedier way to produce bigger specimens with a stronger root system.

Heuchera

Cold frames are useful for rooting cuttings and hardening off

Dividing Perennials

Division of quick-growing herbaceous perennials is a routine maintenance job that can also be turned into a way of propagating more plants. You can divide lifted plants into many small sections as long as they each have some roots. Either replant into replenished soil or pot up in potting compost to encourage new growth. Division is a good way to propagate plants like hostas that increase more steadily and as long as you aren't too greedy in how many individuals you try to make, you can also divide evergreens like *Heuchera* and *x Heucherella* every few years.

How to Divide Plants

Division is best done in spring and autumn, preferably avoiding flowering and hot, dry or frosty periods. You can save money by dividing newly purchased plants, especially any that are pot-bound (not given enough room, causing pot to be full of roots) to create several rooted sections. These are best potted up into compost and grown on for a couple of months before planting out. Dig up clumps for rejuvenation or propagation as follows:

▶ Pick cool, moist conditions.

▶ Use a sharp spade, saw or knife (depending on how tough the rootstock is) to cut off the outer, younger sections.

▶ Discard dead or diseased parts.

Sedum telephium needs regular division

Top Tip

Lever apart dense, hard-to-separate clumps using two border or digging forks back to back. Push the handles away from each other.

▶ Replenish soil by working in several buckets of garden compost or well-rotted manure and a base dressing of general fertilizer.

▶ Replant divisions with space to grow. Or, pot up (see above).

▶ Keep well watered.

235

Sempervivum (house leeks)

Offsets and Runners

Some plants, the classic being house leek (hen and chicks), build up colonies of individuals closely surrounding the mother plant whilst others send out stems that root at intervals and produce plantlets some distance away. By severing these self-propagated plantlets and transferring them to new locations, you can increase stock of favourite plants and make more impact by increasing the size of clumps.

Propagating from Offsets

Typical plant groups that produce offsets include rosette-forming succulents like house leeks (*Sempervivum*) and *Echeveria* and encrusting alpines. Many bulbs including lilies also produce offsets. Look for offsets that have already produced roots. Separate off and plant up in pots of compost (use a gritty mix for succulents).

Rooting Runners

Many ground-cover plants reproduce and spread via runners (overground stems). Strawberries and their ornamental varieties e.g. *Fragaria x ananassa* 'Pink Panda' are good examples – in this case the stems have plantlets at the shoot tips but others may produce them at intervals. Bugle or *Ajuga reptans*, is another classic ground-cover plant. Alternatives for propagation are:

▶ **Moving on:** If plantlets have already started to root, sever from mother plant and pot up or relocate.

236

▶ **Close contact:** Peg plantlets down in close contact with soil or into pots of compost to encourage rooting.

▶ **Potting up:** Sever and pot up young plantlets and keep in sheltered, semi-shaded spot until rooted.

New Plants from Rhizomes

Some plants spread by underground stems or rhizomes that sprout a new tuft of leaves at intervals from the mother plant. Several are invasive in certain soil conditions. Rhizomes are often thick and fleshy, encircling the base of the pot you buy them in. Examples include:

▶ *Anemone x hybrida* (Japanese anemone)
▶ *Convallaria majalis* (lil-of-the-valley)
▶ *Houttuynia cordata* 'Chameleon'
▶ *Macleaya* (plume poppy)
▶ *Matteuchia struthiopteris* (shuttlecock or ostrich fern)
▶ *Mentha* (mints)
▶ *Pleioblastus viridistriatus* (yellow variegated bamboo)

Lily-of-the-valley

Matteuchia struthiopteris (ostrich fern)

237

Rooting Cuttings

Cuttings are surprisingly easy to take and though hardwood cuttings are left in the ground for a year or longer, you will see results from softwood and semi-ripe cuttings pretty quickly. The three main methods are recommended for different times of year when your chances of success are highest. The plant lists, naming good candidates for each method, are not extensive, and it's worth trying a few cuttings of anything you'd like more of, whenever you're in the mood.

Hardwood cutting
with new growth

Hardwood Cuttings

This is the easiest method of rooting shrubs and though it takes a year, plants are larger and garden-ready. It's a great way to propagate lots of material for a new hedge, including ones planted from mixed natives.

General Method

Hardwood cuttings can be taken after leaf fall, in the dormant period (mid autumn to late winter.)

▶ **Length:** Make cuttings 15–30 cm (6–12 in) long from this year's growth. Cut just below a bud or pair of buds – pencil thickness is ideal.

238

▶ **Trim:** Cut off soft growth at the top and any leaves and trim back to just above a bud, using a sloping cut – a useful reminder of which way is up.

▶ **Plant:** Dig a trench, improving soil with organic matter, especially if heavy. Put horticultural sand in the base.

▶ **Distance:** Space out cuttings. Plant with top third protruding and firm in.

Suitable Shrubs and Climbers

The following are all worth trying from hardwood cuttings. Bush roses are usually grafted onto a vigorous rootstock to help with bulk production but grow perfectly well on their own roots.

Escallonia

▶ *Buddleja* (butterfly bush)
▶ *Chaenomeles* (Japanese quince)
▶ *Cornus* (dogwood)
▶ Cotoneaster
▶ *Elaeagnus*
▶ *Escallonia*
▶ *Forsythia*
▶ *Ilex* (holly)
▶ *Ligustrum* (privet)
▶ *Lonicera* (honeysuckle)
▶ *Parthenocissus*
▶ *Rosa* (bush and shrub roses)
▶ *Ribes* (flowering currant)
▶ *Salix* (willow)

▶ *Viburnum*
▶ *Vitis* (vines)
▶ *Weigela*

Parthenocissus

Propagate hydrangea
from shoot tips

Hardwood Cuttings in Containers

You can also root cuttings in pots of 50:50 coarse grit and compost. Keep in a cool, protected spot such as a cold frame. Do not let cuttings dry out. And to kick start slow-to-root cuttings like cornus, try inserting cuttings into a pot filled with moist horticultural sand before transferring to a trench in spring.

Softwood Cuttings

Non-flowering soft shoot tips are raring to go in spring and early summer and cuttings taken then usually root within six to ten weeks. Softwood cuttings can be used to bulk up all kinds of tender perennials including fuchsias, either using overwintered stock plants or buying new potted specimens. The method is also suitable for hardy perennials and numerous climbers including clematis and deciduous shrubs e.g. *Hydrangea macrophylla*.

Rooting in Water

It's fun to root assorted softwood cuttings in a jam jar of water. Place on a shady window ledge. The roots made in water aren't the same as those made in compost, and some cuttings suffer slightly when potted up. Try the following:

- ▶ *Begonia*
- ▶ *Impatiens* (busy Lizzie)
- ▶ *Melissa* (lemon balm)
- ▶ *Mentha* (mint)
- ▶ *Penstemon*
- ▶ *Solenostemon* (coleus)

Rooting in Compost

Collect cuttings in the cool of morning, sealing them in a plastic bag. To prepare:

▶ **Cut:** Using a chopping board and sharp knife, trim, removing lower leaves and cutting just below a bud or pair of buds. Cuttings will be 5–10 cm (2–4 in) long.

▶ **Remove:** Pinch out soft shoot tip.

▶ **Roots:** Dip the cut end in hormone rooting powder/liquid.

▶ **Prepare:** Make a hole in a pot of cutting compost using a pencil/cane (you can fit several cuttings per pot).

▶ **Insert cutting:** The top leaves rest just above soil.

Pinch out the shoot tip when rooted, to promote branching

Top Tip

You can dip the ends in hormone rooting powder. Many root without it but it does contain fungicide which helps prevent rotting.

▶ **Cover:** Firm and water before labelling pot and covering with a clear plastic bag. Place in a warm, light spot or heated propagator. Avoid direct sun.

▶ **Check:** Periodically take off plastic bag for a few minutes and get rid of excess moisture.

▶ **Ventilate:** Once roots start to show through drainage holes, start to increase ventilation by removing the bag for longer periods. Harden off (*see* page 233).

241

Basal Cuttings

This is ideal for perennials that cannot be divided including delphiniums, lupins and salvias. It's also good for Michaelmas daisy (*Aster*), border chrysanthemums and phlox. Pick strong, newly emerging shoots 7–10 cm (3–4 in) long. Cut off as close to the roots as possible. There should be a bit of woodiness at the base of the cutting. Trim off lowest leaves. Pot up and cover with a plastic bag supported with canes as above.

Semi-ripe Cuttings

This type of cutting is taken between late summer and the middle of autumn at a time when the base of cuttings is hard or 'ripe' and the tip is still soft. No special equipment is required but a small electric propagator providing some bottom heat speeds up rooting.

Phlox

Suitable Plants

This is a great way to take cuttings from many evergreen herbs including lavender, rosemary, sage, thyme and bay, as well as evergreen shrubs and hedging plants e.g. box (*Buxus sempervirens*). It can also be used for climbers and wall shrubs such as star jasmine (*Trachelopsermum*) and ceanothus.

Basic Method

Prepare pots with a free-draining mix (50:50 potting compost/perlite or sharp sand). Then:

▶ **Collect:** Put material in a plastic bag.

▶ **Trim:** Take cuttings 10–15 cm (4–6 in) long, just below a leaf bud. Remove lower leaves. Cuttings can be shorter with compact plants like thyme and box.

▶ **Increase chances of rooting:** Try taking heel cuttings (pull away a side shoot from main stem leaving a heel or strip of bark). Trim neatly. Alternatively 'wound' stem at base by cutting off a sliver of bark.

▶ **Relieve stress:** With large leaves like bay, cut them in half to reduce moisture loss.

▶ **Root:** Dip cut end in hormone rooting powder. Tap off excess.

▶ **Plant:** Make a hole for the cutting in the compost and firm in.

▶ **Water:** Use a fine rose spray.

▶ **Cover pots:** Use a plastic bag supported with canes and stand in a light but not sunny spot.

▶ **Keep dry:** If too much moisture builds up on inside of plastic, dry off excess and replace cover.

Box Hedge

If you want to grow enough cuttings to make a box hedge, trimming one piece of topiary such as a box ball in late summer can often give you enough material to plant out the next spring. You can root box cuttings in a shady spot in the ground but if you have a cold frame or can root cuttings under a bench in a warm greenhouse, you can speed things up. Indoors, use a heated propagator for rooting in about eight to ten weeks.

Buxus sempervirens (box)

243

Cotinus (smoke bush)

Layering Shrubs and Climbers

Some shrubs and climbers take root where lower stems have come into contact with the soil. Occasionally you'll find a shrub that has done this already and it's a simple matter to dig up the rooted section and cut it from the parent plant. The layering technique described here just gives nature a helping hand.

Suitable Plants

Many climbers e.g. ivy (*Hedera*), *Hydrangea anomala* supsp. *petiolaris*, golden hop (*Humulus lupulus* 'Aureus'), wisteria and jasmine, and plants that don't take easily from cuttings e.g. Japanese maple (*Acer palmatum*), magnolia, daphne, witch hazel (*Hamamelis*), camellia, rhododendron and azalea and smoke bush (*Cotinus*).

How to Layer

Layer plants in autumn or spring; evergreens preferably in spring. Bend shoot towards the ground and then:

▶ **Make a cut:** About 30 cm (12 in) back from shoot tip, find a leaf bud and make a shallow slanting cut through with a knife. This wounds the stem encouraging callous tissue which produces roots.

▶ **Bury cut:** Push this section down into a depression mixed with grit and compost and cover. Hold down with a brick.

▶ **Provide support:** Bend free end upwards and attach to a vertical cane.

Camellia

244

Checklist

▶ **Seeds:** Collect ripe seed, process and store, or sow immediately. Prepare outdoor seedbeds when soil is workable.

▶ **Out or In:** Thin, weed and water outdoor sowings. Sow half-hardy annuals indoors in warmth (late winter/spring).

▶ **Pricking out:** Prick out seedlings when large enough to handle.

▶ **Hardening off:** Begin to harden off young plants a couple of weeks before last likely frost date.

▶ **Dividing up:** Divide herbaceous perennials (spring or autumn), replanting sections or potting them up.

▶ **Offsets and runners:** Propagate succulents, alpines and lilies from offsets. Separate rooted plantlets from runners. Dig up and relocate plants produced by rhizomes.

▶ **Hardwood:** Root hardwood cuttings of mainly deciduous shrubs, roses and hedging, in a trench outdoors or pots in the cold frame (autumn and winter).

▶ **Softwood:** Take softwood cuttings in spring and early summer.

▶ **Semi-ripe:** Take these cuttings from evergreen herbs, shrubs, box hedging, climbers and wall shrubs, plus tender perennials (late summer through autumn).

▶ **Keep warm:** Provide heat with a propagator or keep warm in a greenhouse.

▶ **Layering:** Layer shrubs and climbers that are tricky to propagate from cuttings (autumn or spring).

Calendar of Care

Early Spring

Pruning and Deadheading

- ☐ Tidy old leaves from spring-flowering evergreen perennials before flowering.
- ☐ Hard prune late-summer-flowering shrubs (not Hydrangea macrophylla). Cut *Santolina*, *Helichrysum italicum*, evergreen *Artemisia* and penstemons back to just above sprouting growth.
- ☐ Shear English lavender if not already done.

General Maintenance

- ☐ Test soil pH to see if lime needed.
- ☐ Apply general fertilizer. Feed roses.
- ☐ Apply/top up bark mulch to reduce weeding.
- ☐ Carry out renovation pruning of overgrown evergreen shrubs.
- ☐ Support taller perennials.
- ☐ Protect emerging shoots of delphiniums, hostas etc. from slugs/snails.

- ☐ Clear annual weeds.
- ☐ Tidy and cut back perennials as new growth emerges.

Planting and Propagation

- ☐ Start sowing half-hardy annuals indoors.
- ☐ Sow *Rudbeckia hirta* varieties under cover for late summer flowering.
- ☐ Divide autumn-flowering herbaceous.
- ☐ Take basal cuttings of delphinium, lupin etc.
- ☐ Finish planting bare-root subjects.
- ☐ Plant snowdrops and winter aconites in-the-green.
- ☐ Pot up summer-flowering bulbs and tubers.

Mid Spring

Pruning and Deadheading

- ☐ Deadhead daffodils etc.
- ☐ Prune forsythia, kerria and flowering currant (*Ribes*) immediately after flowering.

Lightly prune *Hydrangea macrophylla* but keep fleece handy to protect from late frosts.

General Maintenance

- Dig out or spray off problem (perennial) weeds. Choose a still day to avoid spray drift.
- Check shoot tips for aphids.
- Begin watch for lily beetles and their eggs.
- Follow spring bulb deadheading with potassium-rich liquid feed.

Planting and Propagation

- Layer shrubs and climbers.
- Sow first batches of hardy annuals direct once soil is workable.
- Sow most half-hardy bedding and annual climbers indoors.
- Prick out seedlings from earlier sowings.
- Plant Mediterranean herbs, borderline hardy shrubs and evergreens (avoid frost).

Plant perennials, especially autumn-flowering ones.

Late Spring

Pruning and Deadheading

- Cut late-flowering perennials back (Chelsea chop) by $1/3$ to $1/2$ to increase bushiness.
- Begin pruning evergreens. Leave frosted shoots for now as they may recover.
- Deadhead tulips etc.

General Maintenance

- Treat plants suffering nutrient deficiency with sequestered iron and other tonics.
- Liquid-feed plantlets raised from seed or cuttings that show signs of starvation.
- Start hoeing annual weeds.
- Scan for caterpillar and other pests.

Planting and Propagation

- Continue sowing hardy annuals direct.
- Sow hardy biennials in pots under cover or direct in nursery beds (spare ground) for later transplanting to flowering position.

247

- [ ] Weed earlier outdoor sowings, thin and water.
- [ ] Harden off overwintered and softwood cuttings and home-raised bedding.
- [ ] Plant English bluebells (*Hyacinthoides non-scripta*) in-the-green.

Early Summer

Pruning and Deadheading

- [ ] Make first trim of box topiary and hedging (check for bird nests).
- [ ] Deadhead bush, shrub and climbing roses and early perennials.
- [ ] Shear over spring-carpeting plants, feed and water.
- [ ] Lightly prune early, large-flowered clematis after first flush.

General Maintenance

- [ ] Lift bulbs with unsightly foliage and transfer to pots/spare ground.
- [ ] Liquid-feed dahlias and other potted tubers unless using slow-release fertilizer.

Planting and Propagation

- [ ] Make final sowings of hardy annuals direct.
- [ ] Finish sowing hardy biennials like wallflowers.
- [ ] Continue hardening off cuttings and plantlets.
- [ ] Plant out half-hardy bedding, tender perennials and lilies after last frost.

Mid Summer

Pruning and Deadheading

- [ ] Cut back first main spires of delphinium etc. after they've faded to encourage secondary spikes. Deadhead other perennials and roses.
- [ ] Prune or shear certain small-flowered herbaceous, and feed and water, to encourage repeating. Cut *Alchemilla mollis* to prevent seeding and renew foliage.

Cut back over-vigorous ground-cover, foliage shrubs and climbers.

Prune early-summer-flowering shrubs immediately after flowering.

Prune dwarf and trained apple and pear trees, cherries and plums.

Prune frost-damaged evergreens.

General Maintenance

Pick off and destroy black-spot affected rose leaves, mildew and rust-blighted shoots.

Apply biological control and continue pest watch.

Liquid-feed flagging perennials to encourage flowering.

Planting and Propagation

Take semi-ripe cuttings of evergreen shrubs, herbs, box hedging, climbers and wall shrubs.

Plant out dahlias etc. to fill gaps.

Move house and conservatory plants to 'plunge' in borders (acclimatize first).

Late Summer

Pruning and Deadheading

Make final trim of box topiary and hedging.

Cut beech hedges (check for bird nests).

Prune wisteria, cutting back long whip-like shoots to 5–6 leaves.

Shear over English lavender.

General Maintenance

Water flagging plants and ones coming into bloom or with fruit.

Use high potassium liquid feed e.g. comfrey liquor, to increase hardiness of borderline shrubs and climbers.

Planting and Propagation

Begin collecting seed.

Continue taking semi-ripe cuttings, including tender perennials for overwintering.

Plant spring bulbs.

249

Early Autumn

Pruning and Deadheading
- Cut conifer hedges.

General Maintenance
- Move tender specimens back indoors.
- Gather up leaves to make leaf mould.

Planting and Propagation
- Continue collecting seed.
- Begin to layer shrubs and climbers.
- Plant spring- and early-summer-flowering herbaceous.

Mid Autumn

Pruning and Deadheading
- Deadhead late-flowering perennials and roses.

General Maintenance
- Protect recently planted conifers and evergreens with windbreak.
- Lift dahlia, canna and gladioli.
- Continue collecting leaves.

Planting and Propagation
- Take hardwood cuttings.
- Plant spring- and early-summer-flowering herbaceous.

Late Autumn

Pruning and Deadheading
- Lightly prune tall roses, buddleja etc. to prevent wind rock.

General Maintenance
- Begin dormant season renovation pruning of overgrown deciduous shrubs and climbers.
- Tidy dead growth from annual climbers and golden hop. Store herbaceous supports.
- Move any hardy shrubs in the wrong spot.
- Use dry mulches to protect tender tubers etc. left in ground.

Planting and Propagation

- Continue taking hardwood cuttings.
- Begin planting bare-root trees, shrubs, hedging, roses and fruit bushes.

Early Winter

Pruning and Deadheading

- Prune vines and other shrubs and climbers that might 'bleed' sap if cut in spring.

General Maintenance

- Order seeds and plants.
- Bark mulch around borderline hardy evergreen shrubs and perennials.

Planting and Propagation

- Continue to take hardwood cuttings.
- Continue planting bare-root subjects.

Mid Winter

Pruning and Deadheading

- Cut back collapsed stems/rotting flowers creating an eyesore.

General Maintenance

- Insulate frost-vulnerable shrubs, climbers and topiary.
- Top up anti-weed mulch in shrub borders.

Planting and Propagation

- Continue taking hardwood cuttings.
- Continue planting bare-root subjects.

Late Winter

Pruning and Deadheading

- Prune wisteria (*see* page 219).
- Hard prune bush and patio roses and late-flowering clematis (*see* page 219).
- Lightly prune English shrub roses.

General Maintenance

- Refresh paints or stains on fences and trelliswork.
- Add mulches of bulky organic matter and use to improve soil ready for planting.

Planting and Propagation

- Sow sweet peas in pots on the window ledge.
- Finish planting bare-root subjects.

Further Reading

Alexander, R., *The Essential Garden Design Workbook*, Timber Press, 2009

Brickell, C., *The Encyclopedia of Plants and Flowers*, Dorling Kindersley, 2010

DiSabato-Aust, T., *The Well-designed Mixed Garden: Building Beds and Borders with Trees, Shrubs, Perennials, Annuals and Bulbs*, Timber Press, 2003

Fox, R. L., *Thoughtful Gardening: Great Plants, Great Gardens, Great Gardeners*, Particular Books, 2010

Greenwood, P., *The Ultimate Book of Gardening Hints & Tips*, Dorling Kindersley, 2009

Hendy, J., *Garden Decoration: Practical Advice on Adding Interest to Outdoor Spaces, with Containers, Statues, Water Features and Ornaments*, Southwater, 2008

Hendy, J., *Walls, Fences, Hedges and Boundaries: Practical Advice on Designing Garden Barriers and Borders, Using Planting, Wood, Brick, Metal and Ornament*, Southwater, 2008

Hessayon, D. G., *The Pest and Weed Expert*, Expert, 2007

Hobhouse, P., *National Trust Gardening Guides: Borders*, Pavillion Books, 1991

Lord, T., *Best Borders*, Frances Lincoln, 1999

Mikolajski, A., *What to Do When in Your Garden: Plan, Plant and Maintain*, Flame Tree Publishing, 2012

Pavord, A., *Border Book: Illustrated Practical Guide to Planting Borders, Beds and Out-of-the-way Corners*, Dorling Kindersley, 2000

Raven, S., *The Bold and Brilliant Garden*, Frances Lincoln, 2001

Rodale, R., *The Basic Book of Organic Gardening*, Ballantine Books, Inc, 1993

Segall, B., *The Perfect Border: How to Plan, Plant and Maintain the Perfect Border*, Lorenz Books, 2000

Spence, I., *RHS Gardening Through The Year: Your Month-By-Month Guide to what to do when in the Garden*, Dorling Kindersley, 2009

Thomas H. and Wooster, S., Complete Planting Design Course: Plants and Styles for Every Garden, Mitchell Beazley, 2008

Websites

http://www.basicgardentips.com/
If you're just starting out growing things, or if you just have a question that needs answering, this website will steer you and your garden in the right direction.

www.bbc.co.uk/gardening/basics/techniques/
The BBC's gardening homepage provides basic growing techniques for the budding gardener.

www.bhg.com
Better Homes and Gardens magazine's online resource has festive ideas, special tips, and design plans for the perfect home garden.

www.davesgarden.com
Claiming to be the 'hands down favourite website of gardeners around the world', this site offers gardening advice from members' forums and a useful list of approved gardening product companies and websites.

http://www.finegardening.com
This is an online gardening website with lots of articles on design and how-to. Perfect for weekend projects and DIY gardens.

http://www.flower-gardening-made-easy.com/
A web-based resource for maintaining annuals and perennials to make your garden look the best throughout the whole year.

www.gardeners.com
Garden supplies, gardening tools, and gardening tips on all different gardening styles.

http://www.gardenersworld.com
This is a website created by those who produce Gardeners' World magazine, They have a great section of how-to projects and problem solving techniques to help you maintain your garden.

www.gardenweb.com
Hosts a number of logs and forums, as well as articles on gardening and an 'Ask the Experts' section.

http://www.growsonyou.com/
An online community of gardeners, here you can find pictures of thousands of real gardens, links to blogs and a garden centre.

www.lewisgardens.com/beginner.htm
This site offers detailed help for gardening beginners, as well as selling pre-planned garden flower layouts.

www.lovethegarden.com
This well-designed and informative website offers wide-ranging gardening advice about flower, house, vegetable and lawn cultivation, as well as interviews with gardeners and tips on growing flowers.

http://www.organicgardeningguru.com/
A comprehensive resource for gardeners interested in growing organically. Learn tips and tricks, terminology, and how to go green with a green thumb.

www.rhs.org.uk
The Royal Horticultural Society website offering an extensive rage of gardening advice, from cultivation to pest control, as well as a forum allowing you to post personal tips and have your queries answered.

www.suttons,co.uk
Award-winning retailer of seeds and garden equipment. designs for city dwellers who are short of garden space.

Index

256